China's Evolving Approach to "Integrated Strategic Deterrence"

Michael S. Chase, Arthur Chan

For more information on this publication, visit www.rand.org/t/rr1366

Library of Congress Cataloging-in-Publication Data is available for this publication.
ISBN: 978-0-8330-9416-2

Published by the RAND Corporation, Santa Monica, Calif.
© Copyright 2016 RAND Corporation
RAND® is a registered trademark.

Cover: Image shared by Dan via Flickr (CC BY 2.0)

Support RAND
Make a tax-deductible charitable contribution at
www.rand.org/giving/contribute

www.rand.org

Preface

Chinese thinking about strategic deterrence appears to be evolving as China revises its perceptions of its external security environment and improves its military capabilities. First, China's assessment of its external security environment may motivate changes in its thinking about the requirements of "integrated strategic deterrence," a Chinese military concept that calls for a comprehensive and coordinated set of strategic deterrence capabilities, including nuclear, conventional, space, and cyber forces. People's Liberation Army (PLA) strategists appear to regard U.S. "rebalancing" to Asia as part of what they characterize as a broader pattern of U.S. attempts to "contain" China's growing power and influence, and they are concerned about the possibility that improvements in U.S. capabilities—particularly in the areas of missile defense, intelligence, surveillance, and reconnaissance, as well as conventional prompt global-strike capabilities—could undermine the deterrent credibility of China's strategic missile force. Second, the PLA's continued deployment of new and improved capabilities presents Chinese leaders with a wider range of policy and strategy options. For example, at least one important PLA publication, the 2013 edition of *The Science of Military Strategy*, has raised the possibility that, as its early-warning capabilities improve, China may want to adopt a launch-on-warning posture for its nuclear missile force, an option the authors suggest would strengthen deterrence without violating China's nuclear no-first-use policy.

In light of these circumstances, this report looks at China's evolving approach to integrated strategic deterrence. Drawing on a variety of Chinese military writings, this report explores the origins of this concept, how it relates to Chinese development of counter-intervention capabilities, and how Beijing's assessment of its external security environment influences its requirements. We further examine the extent to which improved capabilities create new options for Chinese leaders; how options shape thinking about deterrence; and, on the organizational side, how Chinese leaders will actually integrate disparate instruments of strategic deterrence, some of which are controlled by different services. Finally, the report looks at how competition between the PLA's services has become an important factor in shaping China's strategic deterrence concepts and capabilities and whether Chinese strategists have considered the escalation risks associated with new options. This study should be of interest to analysts, scholars, and policymakers who follow Chinese military affairs and security issues in Asia as well as those engaged in work on nuclear, space, cyberspace, and broader issues of strategic deterrence.

This study was made possible by a generous gift from the Cyrus Chung Ying Tang Foundation. Through this gift, the RAND Center for Asia Pacific Policy established the Tang Institute for U.S.-China Relations in 2007, within which this research was conducted.

RAND Center for Asia Pacific Policy

The RAND Center for Asia Pacific Policy (CAPP) is part of International Programs at the RAND Corporation. CAPP provides analysis on political, social, economic, and technological developments in and around the Asia Pacific. Through research and analysis, CAPP helps public and private decisionmakers solve problems, tackle challenges, and identify ways to make society safer, smarter, and more prosperous.

For more information on the RAND Center for Asia Pacific Policy, see www.rand.org/international_programs/capp or contact the director (contact information is provided on the web page).

Contents

Summary

Drawing on Chinese military writings, this report finds that China's strategic-deterrence concepts are evolving in response to Beijing's changing assessment of its external security environment and a growing emphasis on protecting China's emerging interests in space and cyberspace. At the same time, China is rapidly closing what was once a substantial gap between the People's Liberation Army (PLA's) strategic weapons capabilities and its strategic-deterrence concepts.

Chinese military publications indicate that China has a broad concept of strategic deterrence: It is a multidimensional set of military and nonmilitary capabilities that combine to constitute the "integrated strategic deterrence" posture required to protect Chinese national security interests. This Chinese military concept calls for a comprehensive and coordinated set of strategic-deterrence capabilities. In particular, powerful military capabilities of several types—including nuclear capabilities, conventional capabilities, space capabilities, and cyberwarfare forces—are all essential components of a credible strategic deterrent. The United States also shares this view, as many U.S. strategists see strategic deterrence as encompassing not only the nuclear triad, but also other capabilities, such as long-range conventional strike, cyberspace, missile defense, and space systems. Chinese military publications indicate that nonmilitary aspects of national power—most notably diplomatic, economic, and scientific and technological strength—also contribute to strategic deterrence alongside military capabilities. For Chinese strategists, however, the military components have the most immediate, direct ability to influence a potential adversary's decision-making calculus.

The concept of an integrated strategic deterrent appeared in Chinese military literature around 2001. The broad contours of this idea have remained relatively consistent since, albeit with some elaboration and development over the years, as reflected by more-detailed writings on various aspects of strategic deterrence. These writings reveal a growing emphasis on the PLA's space and information-warfare capabilities, which tracks with China's assessment that military competition in those domains is intensifying.

As the concept of integrated strategic deterrence has evolved to keep pace with China's assessment of its external security environment, emerging interests in space and cyberspace, and changes in military technology, the capabilities supporting it have undergone an impressive transformation. Indeed, some parts of this integrated strategic deterrence concept were initially somewhat aspirational, as China lacked many of the required force structure elements to fully support it. However, Chinese strategic-deterrence capabilities are now rapidly catching up with the ideas embodied in China's concept of integrated strategic deterrence. This is true across the nuclear, conventional, space, and information-warfare domains. China is deploying a more-credible nuclear deterrent comprising improved silo-based intercontinental ballistic missiles (ICBMs) and more-survivable, solid-fueled road-mobile ICBMs and nuclear-powered ballistic missile submarines (SSBNs). Additionally, some publications by PLA Air Force (PLAAF) officers call for modernizing China's ability to deliver nuclear weapons by air. Beijing is also strengthening its conventional military forces, and the air, naval, and missile capabilities most relevant to countering U.S. military intervention provide China with increasingly potent conventional deterrence capabilities. Additionally, Beijing is improving its space and counter-space, cyber-, and electronic-warfare capabilities, which it sees as key components of strategic deterrence and as essential to deterring or fighting modern, information technology–enabled warfare.

As a result of these improvements in nuclear, conventional, space, and information-warfare forces, China's growing strategic-deterrence capabilities increasingly enable it to put its integrated strategic deterrence concepts into practice. Chinese military publications are replete with references to how China can conduct deterrence operations under general peacetime conditions, such as by displaying its strength in military parades and exercises, official and unofficial media reports, satellite imagery, and via the Internet. PLA strategists also discuss higher-intensity deterrence actions that could be conducted to deter U.S. military intervention in a crisis or to reduce the likelihood of further escalation in a conflict scenario, such as raising the readiness level of the strategic missile force, conducting launch exercises, or carrying out information attacks or even limited firepower attacks as a warning.

These developments could have important implications for the United States in a number of areas. In particular, as China continues the development of capabilities to support its integrated strategic deterrence concepts, new capabilities will enable potential changes in Chinese nuclear policies and strategic concepts. Consequently, as China's strategic-deterrence capabilities continue to grow, U.S. analysts will need to watch carefully for signs that Chinese leaders are considering changes to policy and strategy that could be enabled by some of their new capabilities. Even without policy changes, China's further development of its integrated strategic deterrence concepts and capabilities will have implications for strategic stability and escalation management. The United States will need to focus on adopting military responses that are stabilizing and strengthen deterrence, and may need to reduce dependence on capabilities that are potentially highly vulnerable to disruption. The United States will also need to work to build shared understanding with both China and regional allies of the United States by pursuing broader dialogues on strategic deterrence and stability issues that incorporate discussion of relevant nuclear, space, cyberspace, and conventional capabilities. Finally, China's growing strategic weapons capabilities could also create or intensify challenges related to U.S. extended deterrence and assurance of allies. As a result, the United States will likely have to take an increasingly multidimensional approach to extended deterrence and assurance of U.S. allies in the Asia-Pacific region, including new efforts to work with allies to build a common understanding of the threat and developing multidimensional response options.

Acknowledgments

We would like to thank Scott Harold, Rafiq Dossani, and Robin Meili of the RAND Corporation, and Phillip Saunders at the National Defense University, for their peer reviews of the report.

CHAPTER ONE

Introduction

China's requirements for strategic-deterrence capabilities are shaped by key factors including its evaluation of its external security environment and potential threats to its national security and its assessment of changes in military technology, including the growing importance of space and cyberspace. Beijing's evaluation of its external security environment is perhaps the most fundamental of these calculations. Overall, Chinese decisionmakers have a positive view of their external security environment. China's 2015 defense white paper reflects this sentiment: "With a generally favorable external environment, China will remain in an important period of strategic opportunities for its development, a period in which much can be achieved."[1] However, the white paper also specifically points out a number of what China deems as troubling developments in the Asia-Pacific region, including U.S. "rebalancing"; Japan's overhaul of its military and security policies; and what Beijing sees as external interference in China's maritime territorial disputes.[2]

Given China's concerns about their external security environment, it should be no surprise that Chinese military planners are of the opinion that "to forget about [preparing for] war will surely invite

---

[1] "China's Military Strategy [中国的军事战略]," Ministry of National Defense of the People's Republic of China [中华人民共和国国防部], May 2015.

[2] "China's Military Strategy [中国的军事战略]," 2015.

crisis."[3] To that end, China foresees four different kinds of conflicts it might have to face in the future: (1) a large-scale, high-intensity defensive war against a hegemonic country attempting to slow down or interrupt China's rise; (2) a relatively large-scale, relatively high-intensity anti-separatist war against Taiwan independence forces; (3) medium-to-small scale, medium-to-low intensity self-defense counter-operations in territorial disputes or if the internal instability of neighbors spills over Chinese borders; or (4) small-scale, low-intensity operations intended to counter terrorist attacks, preserve stability, and/or preserve the regime.[4] The first possibility—a major war aimed at forestalling China's rise—is the least likely in the view of Chinese strategists, but it is a possibility that they appear not to be completely ruling out. Moreover, the possibility of U.S. military intervention is a serious consideration for China in the second and third types of potential conflict, given that the United States maintains strong unofficial ties with Taiwan and that two of the rival claimants in China's maritime disputes—Japan and the Philippines—are U.S. allies.

This focus on the United States as the main potential adversary that China must be prepared to deter from challenging its interests is not new. For many years, China has viewed the United States as the greatest potential threat to its core national security objectives. This perspective is informed partly by China's perception that the United States is determined to "contain" China or at least to prevent China's rise from challenging its position. It has also been shaped by China's interpretation of a number of specific incidents, such as U.S. involvement in the 1995–1996 Taiwan Strait Crisis, which underscored the likelihood of U.S. military intervention in a cross-strait conflict, and the accidental bombing of the Chinese Embassy in Belgrade by the United States in May 1999, which Chinese leaders viewed as deliberate. The latter incident in particular motivated China to devote even

---

3   Military Strategy Research Department, PLA Academy of Military Science, *The Science of Military Strategy* [战略学], 3rd ed., Beijing: Military Science Press [军事科学出版社], 2013, p. 98.

4   Military Strategy Research Department, PLA Academy of Military Science, 2013, pp. 98–100.

greater resources to improving the capabilities of the People's Liberation Army (PLA) by focusing on asymmetric approaches to exploiting potential U.S. military vulnerabilities and developing advanced, high-technology weapons to deter—or, if necessary, counter—U.S. military intervention in any conflict involving China.[5]

China's strategic-deterrence requirements are also informed by Beijing's analysis of security threats in emerging domains. In particular, Chinese strategists further believe that the PLA needs to be able to protect China's growing interests in space and cyberspace, domains that China sees as challenging because of increasingly sharp international competition. Chinese leaders have called on the PLA to be prepared to cope with potential threats to China's national security interests as they extend into these areas.

In response to these challenges, Chinese security analysts have concluded that China needs a comprehensive, integrated set of strategic-deterrence capabilities. Indeed, Chinese military publications indicate that China has a broad concept of strategic deterrence,[6] in which a multidimensional set of military and nonmilitary capabilities combine to constitute the "integrated strategic deterrence" posture—a Chinese military concept that calls for a comprehensive and coordinated set of strategic-deterrence capabilities, including nuclear, conventional, space, and cyber forces—required to protect Chinese interests.[7] Chi-

---

[5] For more information about the impact of the accidental bombing of the Chinese Embassy in May 1999, see Zhang Wannian, *Biography of Zhang Wannian* [张万年传], Beijing: PLA Press, 2011, pp. 414–421.

[6] A number of articles have focused on individual aspects of China's overall strategic deterrent, such as its nuclear force modernization, space and counter-space, and cyberwarfare capabilities, but little has been published on China's broader concept of strategic deterrence. One important exception is Dennis Blasko, "Military Parades Demonstrate Chinese Concept of Deterrence," *China Brief*, Vol. 9, No. 8, April 16, 2009.

[7] The official dictionary of military terms of the PLA does not contain an entry for "integrated strategic deterrence," but it covers the concepts of military, campaign, intelligence, information, and strategic deterrence, with the latter further divided into the varieties of offensive, defensive, conventional, nuclear, all-out, and limited deterrence. See *People's Liberation Army Military Terms* [中国解放军军语], Beijing: Military Science Academy Press [军事科学出版社], December 2011. *Integrated strategic deterrence* also does not appear in the *Chinese Military Encyclopedia*, although Volume 3 does contain an entry on "strategy of

na's definition of deterrence is also broad in the sense that the Chinese term most often translated as *deterrence*, [*weishe*], has a broader meaning that also encompasses what political science theorists typically refer to as *compellence*.[8] Accordingly, it is perhaps more appropriate to think of *weishe* as roughly equivalent to Thomas Schelling's broader concept of *coercion*, which includes deterrence and compellence.[9] Some Chinese scholars also acknowledge that the meaning of *weishe* is closer to Schelling's broader concept of *coercion*,[10] and discussions of deterrence

---

realistic deterrence," while the Supplemental Volume contains entries on "strategy of limited regional deterrence," "strategy of deterrence," and "strategic deterrence." See *Chinese Military Encyclopedia, Volume 3: Military Academia II* [中国军事百科全书 3: 军事学术 II], Beijing: Military Science Academy Press [军事科学出版社], 1997, and *Chinese Military Encyclopedia, Supplemental Volume* [中国军事百科全书, 增补], Beijing: Military Science Academy Press [军事科学出版社], November 2002. Finally, it does not appear in *Chinese Strategic Missile Force Encyclopedia*, but that encyclopedia does have entries for "nuclear deterrence" and "campaign deterrence." See *Chinese Strategic Missile Force Encyclopedia* [中国战略导弹部队百科全书], Beijing: Chinese Encyclopedia Press [中国百科全书出版社], May 2012. It should also be noted that the term used in the Chinese edition of *The Science of Military Strategy* (SMS) published in 2001 (综合性战略威慑, *zonghexing zhanlue weishe*), might be translated as "comprehensive strategic deterrence" rather than as "integrated strategic deterrence," even though the official English translation released in 2005 uses the latter. Elsewhere, the 2001 edition of SMS uses another term, "integrated deterrence" [整体威慑], which also appears in the 2013 edition of the book. See Peng Guangqian and Yao Youzhi [彭光谦, 姚有志], eds., *The Science of Military Strategy* [战略学], Beijing: Military Science Press [军事科学出版社], 2001, pp. 236, 238, 243; Peng Guangqian and Yao Youzhi, eds., *The Science of Military Strategy*, official English translation of the 2001 Chinese edition, Beijing: Military Science Press, 2005; and Military Strategy Research Department, PLA Academy of Military Science, 2013. Additionally, the Chinese versions of China's defense white papers have used a variety of terms for *deterrence* over the years, including 威慑, 遏制, and 慑止. See, for example, "China's Military Strategy," 2015; "National Defense White Paper: Diversified Uses of China's Military Forces [国防白皮书: 中国武装力量的多样化运用]," Ministry of National Defense of the People's Republic of China [中华人民共和国国防部], April 2013.

[8] See Dean Cheng, "Chinese Views on Deterrence," *Joint Force Quarterly*, No. 60, 1st Quarter, 2011, pp. 92–94.

[9] On the distinctions between *deterrence* and *compellence*, see Thomas C. Schelling, *Arms and Influence*, New Haven, Conn.: Yale University Press, 1966, pp. 69–78.

[10] For example, according to Li Bin, "'weishe' does not mean deterrence; 'weishe' means coercion: to force others to yield to oneself." See Li Bin, "China's Nuclear Strategy," presentation at Carnegie International Nonproliferation Conference, Washington, D.C., June 25–26, 2007.

operations in some Chinese military publications also underscore this point.[11]

Whether the objective is deterrence or compellence, however, one thing that is clear is that Chinese strategists conclude powerful military capabilities of several types—including nuclear, conventional, space, and information warfare—are all essential components of a credible "integrated strategic deterrent."[12] Chinese military publications indicate that nonmilitary aspects of national power, most notably diplomatic, economic, and scientific and technological strength, also contribute to strategic deterrence alongside military capabilities.[13] For Chinese strategists, however, the military components have the most immediate, direct ability to influence a potential adversary's decisionmaking calculus.[14] The concept of an integrated strategic deterrent appeared in Chinese military literature in 2001, and the broad contours of this idea have remained relatively consistent since, albeit with some elaboration and development over the years. The elaborations and developments are reflected by more-detailed writings on various aspects of strategic deterrence as well as a growing emphasis on its space and information

---

[11] See Li Xianyun [李贤允], Rong Jiaxin [容嘉信], Shao Yuanming [邵元明], Ge Xinqing [葛信卿], Huang Zongyuan [黄宗元], Wang Zengyong [王增勇], Chang Jin'an [常金安], Lü Xiangdong, [吕向东], Wang Xiaodong [王晓东], Huang Wei [黄伟], Mao Guanghong [毛光宏], Zhou Min [周敏], Wu Min [武旻], Chen Changming [陈昌明], Li Chaomin [李朝民], *Science of Second Artillery Campaigns* [第二炮兵战役学], Yu Jixun [于际训] and Li Tilin [李体林], eds., Beijing: PLA Press [解放军出版社], March 2004, p. 270. According to this publication, the goal of missile force campaign deterrence operations is to "compel an enemy to accept our will or to contain an enemy's hostile actions." This reflects the broader meaning of *weishe* in that it appears to include not only *deterrence* ("contain an enemy's hostile actions"), but also *compellence* or *coercive diplomacy* ("compel an enemy to accept our will").

[12] See Peng and Yao, 2001, pp. 236, 238, 243.

[13] These other instruments of national power are indispensable because they help to create the optimum conditions for deterrence actions to achieve their political objectives. See Military Strategy Research Department, PLA Academy of Military Science, 2013, p. 135.

[14] Zhao Xijun [赵锡君], ed., *Intimidation Warfare: A Comprehensive Discussion of Missile Deterrence* [慑战: 导弹威慑纵横谈], Beijing: National Defense University Press [国防大学出版社], 2005, pp. 2–3.

components, which tracks with China's assessment that military competition in those domains is intensifying.

As the concept of integrated strategic deterrence has evolved to keep pace with China's emerging interests and changes in military technology, the capabilities supporting it have undergone an impressive transformation. Indeed, at least some parts of this integrated strategic-deterrence concept were initially somewhat aspirational, as China lacked many of the required force structure elements to fully implement the concept. In recent years, however, Chinese capabilities have been rapidly catching up with the conceptual elements of integrated strategic deterrence. This is true across multiple domains. China is deploying a more-credible nuclear deterrent comprising improved silo-based intercontinental ballistic missiles (ICBMs); more-survivable, road-mobile, solid-fueled ICBMs and ballistic missile submarines (SSBNs); and some People's Liberation Army Air Force (PLAAF) officers have advocated for advanced bombers capable of conducting nuclear deterrence and strike missions.[15] Beijing is also strengthening its conventional military forces, and the air, naval, and missile capabilities most relevant to countering U.S. military intervention. These provide China with increasingly potent conventional deterrence capabilities, which constitute an important part of its overall integrated strategic-deterrence posture. Beijing is also improving its space and counter-space, cyber-, and electronic-warfare capabilities, which it sees as key components of strategic deterrence and as essential to protecting its expanding interests in these vital domains.

As a result of these improvements, China's growing capabilities increasingly enable it to employ its integrated strategic deterrence concepts in practice. Chinese military publications are replete with references to how China can conduct deterrence operations under general peacetime conditions, such as by displaying its strength in these areas with military parades and exercises, and through other channels, such as official and unofficial media reports, commercial satellite imagery, and via the Internet. They also discuss actions that could be conducted to deter U.S. military intervention in a crisis or to reduce the likelihood

---

15 Zhu Hui, ed., *Strategic Air Force* [战略空军论], Beijing: Blue Sky Press, 2009.

of further escalation in a conflict scenario, such as raising the readiness level of the strategic missile force, conducting launch exercises, or even carrying out information attacks or limited firepower attacks as a warning.

These developments could have important implications for the United States in a number of areas. In particular, as China continues to develop capabilities to support its integrated strategic deterrence concepts, new options associated with the improved capabilities could lead to modification of existing policies and strategic concepts, such as China's nuclear no-first-use policy and its approach to strategic deterrence operations and nuclear counterattack campaigns. Additionally, China's further development of its integrated strategic deterrence concepts and capabilities will have implications for strategic stability and escalation management. China's growing capabilities could also create or intensify challenges related to U.S. extended deterrence and assurance of allies.

As China's strategic-deterrence capabilities continue to grow, U.S. analysts will need to watch carefully for signs that Chinese leaders are considering changes to policy and strategy that could be enabled by some of their new capabilities. China's growing strategic-deterrence capabilities may also require more-direct U.S. responses in a number of ways. The United States will need to focus on adopting military responses that are stabilizing, such as more-survivable conventional forces, and reduce dependence on capabilities that are potentially vulnerable to disruption. The United States will also need to build shared understanding with both China and regional allies of the United States by pursuing broader dialogues on strategic deterrence and stability issues, which should cover topics and incorporate participants with authority over all of the relevant nuclear, space, cyberspace, and conventional capabilities. At the same time, the United States will likely have to take an increasingly multidimensional approach to extended deterrence and assurance of U.S. allies in the Asia-Pacific region.

The remainder of this report is organized as follows. Chapter Two reviews Chinese strategic-deterrence concepts. Chapter Three presents an overview of China's strategic-deterrence capabilities. Chapter Four examines the implementation of strategic-deterrence actions in peacetime, crisis, and war. Chapter Five offers some conclusions and explores the implications of the study's key findings.

China's Strategic-Deterrence Concepts

Deterrence and warfighting are core functions of China's armed forces, and Beijing's military strategy places as much emphasis on improving its strategic-deterrence capabilities as it does on strengthening its preparations for actual combat. This approach is reflected in a number of publications, including several of China's defense white papers. For example, China's 2008 defense white paper states that China's "military strategic guideline of active defense in the new situation" not only calls for being able to win local wars under "informatized conditions" (which they define as those in which information technology plays a central role and the struggle for information dominance may prove decisive), but it also emphasizes the importance of strategic deterrence.[1] Moreover, the white paper states that, in addition to the development of a "lean and effective" nuclear deterrent force, the military strategic guideline calls for "flexible use of different means of deterrence."[2] Published in 2015, China's most-recent defense white paper focuses on its military strategy, emphasizing deterrence and warfighting, and lists maintaining strategic deterrence as one of the strategic tasks of China's armed forces.[3]

Similarly, according to the 2013 edition of *The Science of Military Strategy* (SMS), an important book on Chinese military strategy

---

[1] "China's National Defense in 2008," Information Office of the State Council, People's Republic of China, January 2009.

[2] "China's National Defense in 2008," 2009.

[3] "China's Military Strategy," 2015.

produced by the Military Strategy Research Department of the PLA's Academy of Military Science, the main objectives of strategic deterrence include deterring the outbreak of war; safeguarding China's maritime sovereignty rights and interests; protecting China's national security interests, including in space and cyberspace; and preserving the "period of strategic opportunity," the 20-year period at the beginning of the century that the Chinese Communist Party's (CCP's) 16th Party Congress in 2002 identified as essential to achieving the party's broader strategic goals.[4]

In pursuit of these objectives, Chinese military publications have discussed integrated strategic deterrence for many years, dating back at least to the 2001 edition of SMS and the English translation of the publication released by China in 2005. Chinese books and journal articles indicate that integrated strategic deterrence is a broad concept that goes well beyond nuclear weapons and even extends beyond military capabilities. The United States has a relatively broad definition of strategic deterrence, which includes a number of different capabilities beyond nuclear weapons, but China's concept is even more expansive in that it encompasses both military and nonmilitary instruments of national power.[5] Indeed, for Chinese strategists, strategic deterrence encompasses political, diplomatic, military, economic, scientific and technological, and informational instruments of national power. Additionally, there are clearly some parallels between Chinese thinking about integrated strategic deterrence and U.S. discussions about "cross-domain deterrence," but China appears to be crafting its own approach in line with its evaluation of what it sees as the most-effective means of addressing the main threats to its national security interests.

Within this broad context, however, PLA authors describe the military element of China's overall strategic-deterrence posture as critical because it is the strongest and most direct means of strategic deter-

---

[4]   Military Strategy Research Department, PLA Academy of Military Science, 2013, pp. 118–119, 143–144.

[5]   Cheryl Pellerin, "Haney: Strategic Deterrence More Than a Nuclear Triad," Washington, D.C.: U.S. Department of Defense (DoD), January 15, 2015.

rence.[6] For example, according to Zhao Xijun, a former deputy commander of PLA Second Artillery Force (PLASAF), China's strategic missile force, military strength is the "main backing and foundation" of strategic deterrence.[7] Similarly, according to SMS 2013, "Military strength, in particular strategic strike strength, is the main body of military deterrence strength, as well as the most basic, direct, and effective factor in carrying out strategic deterrence."[8]

For Chinese strategists, multiple types of military capabilities are relevant to this concept. Chinese military publications indicate that this military component includes China's capabilities across all domains. Most prominently, according to the English version of SMS 2001, which was released in 2005,

> Owing to different national conditions, the strategic deterrence means possessed by different countries are not quite similar. Comprehensive employment of all types of strategic deterrence to give full play to deterrence as a whole for serving national military strategy, however, has been the common option of several countries. China currently possesses a limited but effective nuclear deterrence and a relatively powerful capability of conventional deterrence and a massive capability of deterrence of people's war. By combining these means of deterrence, an integrated strategic deterrence is formed, with comprehensive national power as the basis, conventional force as the mainstay, nuclear force as the backup power and reserve force as the support.[9]

The 2001 edition of SMS also mentions space and information capabilities, but the 2013 edition places much greater emphasis on these areas, reflecting a concept of integrated strategic deterrence

---

[6] Although Chinese military strategists highlight the importance of other elements of national power in terms of China's broader strategic-deterrence posture, the Chinese military publications reviewed for this report do not explain in detail how the contribution of each of these nonmilitary elements to strategic deterrence works in practice.

[7] Zhao, 2005, pp. 2–3.

[8] Military Strategy Research Department, PLA Academy of Military Science, 2013, p. 135.

[9] Peng and Yao, 2005, p. 222.

that depends on a set of complementary and increasingly sophisticated capabilities.

Nuclear Deterrence

Recent Chinese military publications underscore the continuing relevance of nuclear deterrence. Indeed, Chinese military publications suggest that Beijing sees nuclear deterrence as one of the most important forms of strategic deterrence and a cornerstone of its military. For example, according to Zhao, the deterrent effects of nuclear missiles are unmatched by any other weapons, and they are the cornerstone of military deterrence for China.[10] According to the 2013 edition of SMS,

> We should have a profound understanding of the important role played by nuclear strength in ensuring [China's] unwavering status as a great nation, safeguarding core national interests from infringement, and creating a secure environment for peaceful development.[11]

Similarly, Zhao states that the key functions of China's nuclear missile force include serving as an important element of military deterrence, a strong shield for protecting national security, an effective means to deter the outbreak of war, and an important factor in containing the escalation of war.[12]

Because of their destructive power, Chinese strategists see nuclear weapons as useful primarily, if not exclusively, for purposes of strategic deterrence. According to Zhao, if escalation of a war between two nuclear powers results in both sides emptying their nuclear arsenals in retaliation, "the result is mutual destruction," and such a war "cannot achieve meaningful political goals for either side."[13] Consequently, he

---

[10] Zhao, 2005, p. 30.

[11] Military Strategy Research Department, PLA Academy of Military Science, 2013, p. 148.

[12] Zhao, 2005, pp. 29–32.

[13] Zhao, 2005, p. 32.

writes, to a large extent, nuclear weapons have become "pure deterrence weapons."[14] This also means that nuclear deterrence is limited in scope and may have limited relevance in some scenarios, given that it is subject to a number of important restrictions, including national policies and the international strategic environment. Other types of capabilities are therefore required to form a more-comprehensive strategic-deterrence posture.

Conventional Deterrence

Chinese publications highlight the increasing importance of conventional deterrence, which they see as an essential complement to nuclear deterrence. Thinking on this point extends as far back as Zhou Enlai, the first premier of the People's Republic of China (PRC), who once argued that conventional and nuclear arms both have their uses. The latter cannot replace the former, and even after development of nuclear arms has reached a certain level, conventional arms cannot be neglected.[15] Recent Chinese military publications suggest that, although conventional military deterrence is not as powerful as nuclear deterrence, it is becoming more important as conventional weapons become more capable.[16] Indeed, PLA strategists indicate that the power of conventional deterrence is growing with the "informatization" of conventional strike capabilities. For example, the 2013 edition of SMS notes that improvements in conventional weapons capabilities have dramatically increased the deterrence strength of conventional military power after the Cold War. Additionally, PLA publications on strategy suggest that conventional military deterrence is applicable to a wider range of circumstances than nuclear deterrence. For instance, the 2013 edition of

---

[14] Zhao, pp. 36, 214.

[15] Quoted by Sun Xiangli, in Gong Ting [龚婷], ed., "Nuclear, Fifty Years in China [核，来到中国50年]," China Institute of International Studies [中国国际问题研究院], October 21, 2014.

[16] Military Strategy Research Department, PLA Academy of Military Science, 2013, pp. 137–138.

SMS contends that conventional weapons are more usable and offer much greater flexibility than nuclear weapons. Moreover, according to the 2013 edition of SMS, as a result of the powerful capabilities of advanced conventional weapons and the fact that they are not subject to the unique constraints associated with nuclear weapons, modern conventional weapons are becoming "a powerful deterrence means for achieving political objectives."[17]

Space and Cyberspace Deterrence

PLA and CCP publications indicate that China sees space and cyberspace as increasingly important arenas for strategic deterrence, along with the expansion of China's interests—and potentially vulnerabilities—in these areas. For instance, Liang Yabin, writing for the Central Party School's *Study Times*, has advocated democratizing Internet governance through the United Nations and challenging U.S. hegemony in this domain.[18] If achieved, this would be a step toward China's oft-repeated goal of fostering a multipolar world at the expense of the United States. Moreover, according to PLA analysts and strategists, space and cyberspace are not only increasingly important, but also increasingly contested domains. The 2015 "Military Strategy" white paper, for example, refers to both space and cyberspace as new high grounds in the strategic competition between countries.[19] A member of the PLA General Staff Department's Third Department, which is responsible for signals intelligence (SIGINT) and cyberespionage, also has noted the fierce competition between various countries—including the United States, Japan, the United Kingdom, Germany, Russia, and Canada—initiated in cyberspace, in space, and at the geographic poles in their respective

---

[17]   Military Strategy Research Department, PLA Academy of Military Science, 2013, p. 137.

[18]   Liang Yabin [梁亚滨], "Network Space Is the New Domain for National Competition in the Big Data Era [网络空间是大数据时代国家博弈的新领域]," *Study Times* [学习时报], October 20, 2014.

[19]   "China's Military Strategy," 2015.

efforts to seize the strategic initiative in these domains.[20] In regard to the contest for space dominance, SMS 2013 asserts that this competition has already been underway for many decades, and since the beginning of the 21st century, "military struggle in the space domain" has intensified, thus increasing the challenges associated with the protection of China's growing interests in space.[21] Similarly, in cyberspace, PLA strategists and CCP thinkers see the stakes rising and competition between major powers intensifying as countries become increasingly dependent on computer networks for a wide variety of military and economic functions.[22] Indeed, according to PLA strategists, a "sharp struggle" has already begun to unfold in the network domain, with states contending over information security in peacetime and preparing to seize the initiative by struggling to gain "network dominance" over their adversaries in wartime.[23] Moreover, Chinese strategists see the United States and other countries with powerful military forces as seeking to gain new advantages in these areas by pursuing space and cyberwarfare capabilities that could threaten Chinese interests. A June 2015 editorial in the *Study Times*, a publication run by the Central Party School, made such an argument. It takes a dim view of U.S. attempts to use the North Atlantic Treaty Organization to "revive its own flagging fortunes," increase cyber-based cooperation with Japan and Australia, and remake the "virtual" international order. In particular, the piece refers to the latter as "squeezing" China's national interests in cyberspace.[24]

---

[20] Li Li [李莉], "A New Space for Strategic Competition [战略博弈新空间]," World Knowledge [世界知识], 2011.

[21] Military Strategy Research Department, PLA Academy of Military Science, 2013, p. 179.

[22] Ye Zheng [叶征], "On Essential Characteristics, Force Composition and Content Form of Strategic Competition in Cyberspace [论网络空间战略博弈的本质特征，力量构成与内容形式]," People.cn, Theory Channel [人民网－理论频道], August 18, 2014.

[23] Military Strategy Research Department, PLA Academy of Military Science, 2013, pp. 188–189.

[24] "America's Cyberspace Strategy Shifting to 'Strategic Deterrence and Offensive Operations' [美国网络空间战略正向"战略威慑和进攻行动"转变]," *Study Times* [学习时报], 2015.

At the same time, space and cyberspace are also domains that afford China some opportunities to strengthen and expand the scope of its own strategic deterrence posture. According to the 2013 edition of SMS,

> since entering the 21st century, along with the rapid development and widespread application of science and technology, especially information technology, the Internet and space are gradually developing into new strategic deterrence domains, allowing strategic deterrence to comprehensively utilize many types of deterrence methods.[25]

More concretely, according to the same book, the development of military space forces

> consolidates and boosts [China's] strategic deterrence capability; ensures an important support for the expansion of state interests; and is of important significance for building informatized armed forces, for winning informatized wars, and for pushing forward the PLA's strategic transformation.[26]

Space forces and space deterrence play important roles not only in crisis or conflict situations, when they can be used to send focused and clearly directed deterrence signals, but even in peacetime, when

> the existence and development of one side's space systems, and the elevation of its space capabilities, can potentially influence and constrain the military activity of other nations, and thus generate certain deterrent effects.[27]

Network warfare capabilities can also bolster strategic deterrence, and PLA strategists identify *network deterrence*, a term they employ roughly in the way *cyber deterrence* is used in the United States, as one

---

[25] Military Strategy Research Department, PLA Academy of Military Science, 2013, pp. 228–229.

[26] Military Strategy Research Department, PLA Academy of Military Science, 2013, p. 179.

[27] Military Strategy Research Department, PLA Academy of Military Science, 2013, p. 182.

of three "main patterns of military struggle in the network domain," along with "network reconnaissance" and "network attack and defense operations."[28] However, they argue that "network deterrence" is different than traditional strategic deterrence in many respects. In particular, according to SMS 2013,

> Although deterrence is an important aspect of military struggle in the network domain, there is nonetheless very great diversity in different people's understandings of network deterrence, and the theory and practice of network deterrence both await further development and perfection.[29]

The authors of SMS do not further develop this point, but this would seem to increase the risks· of misperception and misinterpretation of actions in the network domain, potentially leading to inadvertent escalation.

---

[28] Military Strategy Research Department, PLA Academy of Military Science, 2013, pp. 192–194.

[29] Military Strategy Research Department, PLA Academy of Military Science, 2013, p. 194.

CHAPTER THREE

China's Strategic-Deterrence Capabilities

China has devoted considerable attention to developing the capabilities required to support the concept of integrated strategic deterrence. This appears to reflect determination on the part of China's top leaders to build a powerful strategic deterrent based on modern forces. Indeed, when Jiang Zemin served as General Secretary of the Chinese Communist Party from 1989 to 2002, he called upon the PLA to develop a "strategic deterrence system" comprising multiple types of capabilities.[1] More recently, SMS 2013 stated

> Future preparations for military struggle must not only strive to enhance the capability to win local wars, but also strive to establish and strengthen a military deterrence system and military deterrence capabilities that are capable of deterring the outbreak of war and preventing the escalation of war.[2]

Specifically, SMS 2013 states that the PLA's "deterrence system" should include the following five types of capabilities:

- "Lean and effective nuclear strike forces" (China's land- and sea-based nuclear forces)
- "Informatized conventional operations forces" (China's conventional military forces, which are increasingly supported by

---

[1] Military Strategy Research Department, PLA Academy of Military Science, 2013, pp. 142–143.

[2] Military Strategy Research Department, PLA Academy of Military Science, 2013, p. 134.

advanced intelligence, surveillance, and reconnaissance [ISR], communications, and command automation capabilities)
- "Information attack and defense forces with local superiority" (China's offensive and defensive cyber- and information-warfare capabilities)
- "Flexible and diverse space strength" (China's space and counterspace capabilities)
- "Innovatively developed integrated deterrence strength of people's war" (China's ability to leverage civilian resources to facilitate military modernization and support military operations).

China's strategic-deterrence capabilities were relatively limited in each of these areas when the concept of integrated strategic deterrence was articulated in SMS 2001. Most prominently, China possessed a small and potentially vulnerable nuclear force comprising a small number of silo-based ICBMs and theater missiles. China's long-range conventional strike capabilities were limited, as it had deployed a small number of relatively inaccurate conventional missiles. China's space capabilities also were relatively modest. Although China's capabilities were quite limited at the time the concept of integrated strategic deterrence appeared in SMS 2001, much has changed in the past 15 years. Indeed, China has made impressive strides in nuclear, conventional, space, and information warfare, and it is continuing to strengthen its capabilities in each of these areas. The following sections provide brief overviews of Chinese nuclear, conventional strike, space and counterspace, and cyber- and electronic-warfare (EW) capabilities, all of which are essential components of the broader "deterrence system" described in recent Chinese military publications.

China's Nuclear Forces

Chinese strategists view nuclear weapons as the cornerstone of China's broader strategic deterrence. SMS 2013 states that China should understand that nuclear forces play an "important role" in "ensuring [China's] status as a great power is unwavering, safeguarding the nation's core interests from infringement, and creating a secure environment for peaceful development."[3]

Furthermore, SMS 2013 emphasizes the importance of developing a "limited, but effective nuclear force," which it describes as an essential "pillar" of the PLA's broader "deterrence system."[4] Accordingly, Beijing is modernizing its nuclear force to ensure it will have an assured retaliatory capability. Chinese strategists argue this is essential because of concerns that U.S. missile defense, ISR, and conventional strike capabilities could undermine the credibility of China's nuclear deterrence.[5]

Although China's strategic nuclear force remains relatively small (consisting of about 50–75 ICBMs), Beijing is improving it along several dimensions.[6] In particular, China has equipped some of its DF-5 silo-based ICBMs with multiple, independently targetable reentry vehicles (MIRV), and the PLASAF continues to deploy more-survivable, road-mobile ICBMs.[7] Additionally, China is deploying a sea-based nuclear deterrent with the PLA Navy's (PLAN) Type 094 SSBNs and the associated JL-2 submarine-launched ballistic missiles (SLBM).

China continues to emphasize improving its nuclear deterrent, as reflected by the 2015 military strategy white paper's references to the PLAN and PLASAF improving their capabilities for strategic deterrence and nuclear counterattack, and its statement that China

> will optimize its nuclear force structure, improve strategic early warning, command and control, missile penetration, rapid reac-

---

[3]   Military Strategy Research Department, PLA Academy of Military Science, 2013, p. 148.

[4]   Military Strategy Research Department, PLA Academy of Military Science, 2013, p. 148.

[5]   Jeffrey Lewis, "China's Nuclear Modernization: Surprise, Restraint, and Uncertainty," in Ashley J. Tellis, Abraham M. Denmark, and Travis Tanner, eds., *Strategic Asia 2013–14: Asia in the Second Nuclear Age*, Seattle, Wash.: National Bureau of Asian Research, October 2013, pp. 67–96.

[6]   U.S. Department of Defense, *Annual Report to Congress: Military and Security Developments Involving the People's Republic of China 2013*, Washington, D.C.: Office of the Secretary of Defense, May 2015, p. 31.

[7]   DoD, 2015, p. 8.

tion, and survivability and protection, and deter other countries from using or threatening to use nuclear weapons against China.[8]

Similarly, SMS 2013 highlights the importance of improving informatization, command and control, strategic early warning, mobility, "rapid response capability," penetration capability, and survivability, in order to further increase the credibility of nuclear deterrence.[9] Similarly, another important source, *China's Strategic Missile Force Encyclopedia*, highlights the importance of improving missile force survivability through maneuverability, concealment, and rapid response time.[10] It also discusses the importance of being able to penetrate enemy missile defense systems through means such as multiple warhead technology, maneuvering warheads, decoys, stealth, and saturation attacks.[11]

As usual, Chinese publications such as SMS 2013 do not discuss the details of systems currently under development or Chinese force modernization plans, but the general guidance that appears in such books aligns with outside assessments of China's development of a number of new capabilities. For PLASAF, perhaps the most important of these is the DF-41, a road-mobile ICBM that may be capable of carrying MIRVs. China is also developing and testing a hypersonic-glide vehicle,[12] which appears to be a very high priority program as reflected by the four flight tests of the system China conducted between January 2014 and June 2015.[13] Additionally, PLAN is widely expected to develop and deploy a next-generation SSBN, called the Type 096, and

---

[8] "China's Military Strategy," 2015.

[9] Military Strategy Research Department, PLA Academy of Military Science, 2013, p. 148.

[10] See *Chinese Strategic Missile Force Encyclopedia*, 2012, pp. 73, 77–78.

[11] See *Chinese Strategic Missile Force Encyclopedia*, 2012, p. 87.

[12] For an in-depth analysis of related issues, see Lora Saalman, "Prompt Global Strike: China and the Spear," Honolulu, Hawaii: Asia-Pacific Center for Security Studies, April 2014.

[13] See, for example, Zachary Keck, "Why America Should Fear China's Hypersonic Nuclear Missile," *The National Interest*, June 15, 2015.

a new SLBM, to strengthen the sea-based component of its nuclear deterrent.[14]

China's missile defense program could also be seen as a means of enhancing the credibility of its nuclear deterrent, even though Chinese officials and scholars have long objected to the United States developing its own missile defense capabilities. Fan Jishe of the Chinese Academy of Social Sciences and Sun Xiangli of the Chinese Academy of Engineering Physics, for example, have argued that U.S. national missile defense could lead to arms races and strategic instability.[15] Presumably the same could happen if China decided to develop its missile defense capabilities, but Chinese scholars suggest the utility of missile defense for deterrence depends on how it is deployed and the purpose for which it is intended. Li Bin of the Carnegie-Tsinghua Center expands on this point in a 2013 article responding to China's second missile intercept test. He notes that

> China worries that U.S. missile defense will undermine its deterrent capability and therefore erode U.S.-Chinese strategic stability. The United States emphasizes that it does not intend to weaken China's deterrent capability but does not explain what limitations in the capabilities of its missile defenses prevent it from doing so.[16]

Because of this and other considerations, Li cautions against China investing in its own national missile defense system because it will have a similarly negative effect on strategic stability between the two countries. He instead suggests a point defense system as more

---

[14] DoD, 2015.

[15] Fan Jishe, "The Effect of a National Missile Defense System on the Global Security Structure [国家导弹防御系统对全球战略格局的影响]," Chinese Academy of Social Sciences [中国社会科学院], March 15, 2001; Gong, 2014.

[16] Li Bin, "What China's Missile Intercept Test Means," Carnegie Endowment for International Peace, February 4, 2013.

feasible and capable of increasing the survivability of China's nuclear weapons. He argues,

> In such a way, a point defense system would make China's nuclear deterrent more credible and ensure its strategic stability with other nuclear-armed countries.[17]

In all, China is enhancing the striking power and survivability of its theater and strategic nuclear missile forces and improving their ability to counter enemy missile defense systems.[18] These developments are giving China a much more credible nuclear deterrent based on a secure second-strike capability. These improvements to Chinese nuclear forces are broadly consistent with China's desire to build a lean and effective nuclear deterrent. They also allow China's nuclear forces to serve as the cornerstone of its overall integrated strategic deterrence posture.[19]

PLA Conventional Forces

China's conventional military capabilities, particularly high-end capabilities relevant to deterring or countering U.S. military intervention, also constitute an important part of China's integrated strategic deterrence. Chinese strategists suggest that the importance of conventional deterrence is growing. They argue that conventional deterrence is becoming more prominent not only because of improvements in conventional precision-strike capabilities, but also as a result of the higher credibility of conventional threats in a wider range of scenarios and the greater flexibility associated with their actual employment compared with nuclear weapons. For China, the conventional capabilities that likely make the strongest contribution to its integrated strategic

---

[17] Li Bin, 2013.

[18] Michael S. Chase, Andrew Erickson, and Chris Yeaw, "Chinese Theater and Strategic Missile Force Modernization and Its Implications for the United States," *Journal of Strategic Studies*, Vol. 32, No. 1, 2009, pp. 67–114.

[19] Michael S. Chase, "China's Transition to a More Credible Nuclear Deterrent: Implications and Challenges for the United States," *Asia Policy*, Vol. 16, 2013, pp. 69–101.

deterrence-posture include weapons deployed with the PLASAF, such as anti-ship ballistic missiles, conventional medium-range ballistic missiles, and land-attack cruise missiles, PLAAF bombers equipped with air-launched cruise missiles, and PLAN submarines and surface ships equipped with long-range anti-ship cruise missiles.[20] China is continuing to develop and improve its conventional deterrence posture, as reflected by the development of a conventional intermediate-range ballistic missile for the PLASAF and efforts by the PLAAF and PLAN to strengthen their conventional strike capabilities.[21] This is in line with PLA publications such as SMS 2013, which calls for the PLA to develop "informatized" conventional forces with advanced command, control, communications, computers, intelligence, surveillance and reconnaissance, and long-range precision strike capabilities.[22]

On the whole, China has made dramatic strides in improving its conventional military capabilities, which has important implications for strategic deterrence. Indeed, the long-range conventional strike systems it has deployed to hold at-risk targets such as regional air bases and surface ships do more than improve China's ability to conduct military operations along its maritime periphery and to counter U.S. military intervention. They also allow PLA conventional forces to make an increasingly powerful contribution to China's overall integrated strategic-deterrence posture.[23]

---

[20] DoD, 2015.

[21] See U.S. Navy, *The PLA Navy: New Capabilities and Missions for the 21st Century*, Washington, D.C.: Office of Naval Intelligence, 2015; DoD, 2015; and Richard P. Hallion, Roger Cliff, and Phillip C. Saunders, eds., *The Chinese Air Force: Evolving Concepts, Roles, and Capabilities*, Washington, D.C.: National Defense University, 2012.

[22] Military Strategy Research Department, PLA Academy of Military Science, 2013, p. 148.

[23] For a recent assessment of these capabilities, see Eric Heginbotham, Michael Nixon, Forrest E. Morgan, Jacob Heim, Jeff Hagen, Sheng Li, Jeffrey Engstrom, Martin C. Libicki, Paul DeLuca, David A. Shlapak, David R. Frelinger, Burgess Laird, Kyle Brady, and Lyle J. Morris, *The U.S.-China Military Scorecard: Forces, Geography, and the Evolving Balance of Power, 1996–2017*, Santa Monica, Calif: RAND Corporation, RR-392-AF, 2015.

Information-Warfare Capabilities

China is making impressive strides in its information-warfare capabilities, including developments related to computer network operations.[24] Chinese cyber capabilities could help the PLA gather information for intelligence purposes or conduct cyberattacks more effectively. According to DoD, such attacks "can be employed to constrain and adversary's actions to slow response time by targeting network-based logistics, communications, and commercial activities."[25] They could also be employed in coordination with conventional strikes to help the PLA achieve "information dominance" by denying an adversary the ability to rely on its computer networks and information systems. In addition, the PLA sees EW as an important means of reducing a high-technology adversary's advantage in a conflict with China. EW could be employed along with conventional and cyberattacks to target enemy radars and other electronic equipment. China is researching and deploying offensive and defensive EW capabilities to its forces and testing them in simulations and exercises.[26]

SMS 2013 highlights the importance of continuing to improve Chinese information warfare capabilities and further strengthening their contribution to China's overall "deterrence system." According to SMS, the PLA must "insist on practicing active information defense strategically," but it must develop offensive capabilities as well as improving its defenses. Specifically, SMS 2013 states

> on the basis of continuously enhancing information network system defense capability, [the PLA must] speed up building information operations units that employ information warfare weapons and equipment as the main operational means and spe-

---

[24] James Mulvenon, "PLA Computer Network Operations: Scenarios, Doctrine, Organizations, and Capability," in Roy Kamphausen, David Lai, and Andrew Scobell, eds., *Beyond the Strait: PLA Missions Other than Taiwan*, Carlisle, Pa.: U.S. Army War College, Strategic Studies Institute, April 2009, pp. 253–286; and Joe McReynolds, "China's Evolving Perspectives on Network Warfare," *China Brief*, Vol. 15, No. 8, April 16, 2015.

[25] DoD, 2015, p. 37.

[26] DoD, 2015, p. 38.

cialize in carrying out information warfare tasks; and strive to develop diversified information operations attack and defense means to effectively guard against and deter an enemy from initiating a large-scale information invasion.[27]

Evaluating the degree to which China's cyber- and electronic-warfare capabilities contribute to strengthening its integrated strategic deterrence posture may be an impossible task due to the fact that the PLA, like most other militaries, does not publicly release information about what it probably sees as some of its most sensitive capabilities. Apart from secrecy, other complicating factors include appropriate measures of effectiveness in this area. It seems reasonable to suggest that PLA cyber- and electronic-warfare capabilities could contribute to strategic deterrence directly—such as by using cyberwarfare capabilities against critical infrastructure targets—as well as indirectly, by enabling China to more effectively employ its conventional military capabilities.

Chinese Space and Counter-Space Capabilities

China's 2015 white paper on military strategy highlights the growing importance of space, which it highlights as "a commanding height in international strategic competition." Furthermore, the paper states that

> Countries concerned are developing their space forces and instruments, and the first signs of weaponization of outer space have appeared. China has all along advocated the peaceful use of outer space, opposed the weaponization of and arms races in outer space, and taken an active part in international space cooperation. China will keep abreast of the dynamics of outer space, deal with security threats and challenges in that domain, and secure its space assets to serve its national economic and social development, and maintain outer space security.[28]

---

[27] Military Strategy Research Department, PLA Academy of Military Science, 2013, p. 148.

[28] "China's Military Strategy," 2015.

Although the white paper highlights the importance of space and the priority China attaches to protecting its space security, it offers no further information on the development of China's military space and counter-space capabilities. Nonetheless, a variety of reports from the United States and other countries highlight the priority China clearly attaches to further developing its military space and counter-space capabilities.[29]

China has invested substantial resources in the development of a number of types of satellites with military applications, including ISR; positioning, timing, and navigation; and communications systems. China is also improving its ground infrastructure and space-launch capabilities, most notably with the completion of the Wenchang Space Launch Center on Hainan Island (China's fourth space-launch center), improvements in space-surveillance capabilities, and the development of new types of space-launch vehicles.[30]

China also has a multidimensional program to develop counter-space capabilities. According to DoD, China "continues to develop a variety of capabilities designed to limit or prevent the use of space-based assets by adversaries during a crisis or conflict."[31] These capabilities include the direct ascent anti-satellite (ASAT) system China used in a January 2007 test that destroyed a defunct weather satellite and created a large amount of space debris. In July 2014, China conducted another test of this system, which is designed to destroy satellites in low Earth orbit, but the July 2014 test did not create any space debris.[32] Additionally, China appears to be developing capabili-

[29] Kevin Pollpeter, "Controlling the Information Domain: Space, Cyber, and Electronic Warfare," in Ashley J. Tellis and Travis Tanner, eds., *Strategic Asia 2012–13: China's Military Challenge*, Seattle, Wash.: National Bureau of Asian Research, October 2012, pp. 162–194; Ashley J. Tellis, "China's Military Space Strategy," *Survival*, Vol. 49, No. 3, September 2007, pp. 41–72; and Michael Krepon, "China's Military Space Strategy: An Exchange," *Survival*, Vol. 50, No. 1, February–March 2008, pp. 157–198; Michael S. Chase, "Defense and Deterrence in China's Military Space Strategy," *China Brief*, Vol. 11, No. 5, March 25, 2011.

[30] DoD, 2015, pp. 13–14.

[31] DoD, 2015, p. 14.

[32] China characterized the July 2014 test of this system as a missile defense test, but DoD reports that it was actually a test of the missile system Beijing tested in January 2007, which

ties to attack satellites in geosynchronous Earth orbit.[33] Specifically, in May 2013, China conducted a space launch that may have involved "a test of technologies with a counter-space mission in geosynchronous orbit," according to DoD.[34] China's counter-space efforts also include "the development of directed-energy weapons and satellite jammers."[35] China has also demonstrated the ability to maneuver satellites in close proximity, a requirement for co-orbital ASAT systems,[36] as well as space robotic-arm technology that could have military applications.[37]

In addition, other Chinese military capabilities could be relevant to space deterrence or counter-space operations. For example, China's cyberwarfare and long-range conventional strike capabilities could be used to target satellite ground stations.[38]

China's development of its military space capabilities, particularly its development of several different types of counter-space systems, appears designed to create the "flexible and diverse space strength" PLA strategists envision as a key component of China's broader "com-

---

is designed to destroy targets in low Earth orbit. See DoD, 2015, p. 35.

[33] Brian Weeden, "Through a Glass, Darkly: Chinese, American, and Russian Anti-Satellite Testing in Space," Broomfield, Colo.: Secure World Foundation, March 17, 2014.

[34] DoD, 2015, p. 14. Beijing said the launch was for scientific research, but many observers believe it was an anti-satellite test. According to the DoD report:

> On May 13, 2013, China launched an object into space on a ballistic trajectory with a peak altitude above 30,000 km. This trajectory took it near geosynchronous orbit, where many nations maintain communications and earth-sensing satellites. Analysis of the launch determined that the booster was not on the appropriate trajectory to place objects in orbit and that no new satellites were released. The post-boost vehicle continued its ballistic trajectory and re-entered Earth orbit 9.5 hours after launch. The launch profile was not consistent with traditional space-launch vehicles, ballistic missiles or sounding rocket launches used for scientific research.

[35] DoD, 2015, p. 14.

[36] Dean Cheng, "The PLA's Interest in Space Dominance: Testimony Before U.S.-China Economic and Security Review Commission," Washington, D.C.: The Heritage Foundation, February 18, 2015.

[37] Kevin Pollpeter, "China's Space Robotic Arm Programs," *SITC Bulletin Analysis*, San Diego, Calif.: University of California, San Diego, Institute on Global Conflict and Cooperation, October 2013.

[38] Cheng, 2015.

prehensive strategic deterrent." Specifically, according to SMS 2013, the PLA should

> regard having the capabilities to support free utilization of space as well as to accomplish strategic early-warning and strategic reconnaissance tasks with high efficiency as the core; accelerate the enhancement of space information support capabilities, information defense capability, and information control capability; strengthen our own counter-strike, counter-interference, and counter-destruction capabilities; and continue to enhance the capability to safeguard China's space security, so as to effectively contain and deter the enemy's intention of conducting space deterrence and attack against China.[39]

Other areas of emphasis in the future for the development of PLA space and counter-space capabilities are likely to include improved space situational awareness; a rapid space-launch capability similar to the U.S. concept of "operationally responsive space"; and offensive and defensive space-control capabilities, particularly those designed to achieve "mission kills," such as co-orbital jammers and cyber- and information-warfare capabilities.[40]

Other Chinese military publications have emphasized the importance of space-based capabilities as key components of "new joint operations of the future."[41] A 2012 article in *China Military Science*, one of the PLA's most important professional military journals, states that the core advantage of outer space in current military affairs is providing information integration support. However, this will change with the development and improvement of aerospace weapons equipment. Because of this, the article urges continual reform and innovation in order to seize the high ground in outer-space operational theory, with particular emphasis on "understanding outer space, using outer space,

---

[39] Military Strategy Research Department, PLA Academy of Military Science, 2013, p. 148.

[40] Cheng, 2015.

[41] Yue Guiyun, Chen Xiaoyang, and Li Jingxu, "Considerations on Some Important Issues on New Joint Operations in the Future [未来新型联合作战若干重要问题思考]," *China Military Science* [中国军事科学], 2012, pp. 134–136.

defending outer space, and fighting in outer space." At the same time, the article urges the strong development of an outer-space information counter-measures system, as "an information advantage depends on an outer space advantage, and without control of outer space, there can be no control of the sky, seas or land."[42]

As with its nuclear and conventional forces, China has clearly devoted substantial resources to improving its space and counter-space capabilities, which it sees as relevant not only to seizing the initiative and winning the struggle for information dominance in possible future conflicts, but also as making an important and growing contribution to its overall integrated strategic deterrence posture. Chinese strategists probably believe their increasingly impressive space and counter-space capabilities could deter an adversary both by demonstrating the ability to damage or destroy strategically important and expensive space systems and by threatening the enemy's ability to use those systems to successfully carry out its own conventional military operations.

"People's War" and Deterrence

Finally, some Chinese military publications mention another factor that complements nuclear, conventional, space, and cyber capabilities and contributes to strategic deterrence: "People's war" is a concept typically associated more with the PLA of the Mao Zedong era than with today's increasingly high-tech Chinese military. Although it might be tempting to dismiss discussions of the relevance of "people's war" in this context as little more than a form of PLA political correctness, Chinese strategists appear to view it as a factor that contributes to strategic deterrence in important ways. In particular, Chinese strategists see "people's war" in terms of the potential to leverage improvements in civilian scientific and technological capabilities in support of military modernization and, if necessary, to mobilize civilian resources more directly to support military operations. Indeed, "people's war" was a key element of the integrated strategic deterrence posture described

---

[42] Yue, Chen, and Li, 2012, pp. 134–136.

in SMS 2001, and more-recent Chinese military publications—most notably SMS 2013—continue to portray "people's war" as an important component of China's overall strategic-deterrence posture. According to that book, "China's military deterrence emphasizes a comprehensive application of various strengths, and gains a foothold in the application of overall strength, which includes people's war."[43] Specifically, SMS 2013 states that incorporating this concept into a contemporary strategic-deterrence framework requires China to establish an efficient and responsive capacity to enable mobilization of the nation's war potential.[44] Additionally, according to the same book, enhancing "military-civilian fusion" can help strengthen China's integrated strategic deterrence posture by providing "an even more solid material and technological foundation" for Chinese military modernization, thus "expanding the connotation of the deterrence function of people's war under informatized conditions."[45] Before this, as early as 2000, PLA analysts had advocated the creation of a military-civilian compatible support system, which could provide logistical support to troops in both peace and wartime, potentially to great military and economic effect.[46] The PLA continues to advocate developing military-civilian fusion as a form of strategic deterrence but stresses the need for high-tech weapons, a quick mobilization process, increased technical know-how among the population, and flexible methods to deal with new challenges in the age of informatization.[47] Although some sources suggest the deterrent effects of "people's war" are manifest primarily in China's ability to mobilize rapidly for a short duration conflict, it would

---

[43] Military Strategy Research Department, PLA Academy of Military Science, 2013, p. 145.

[44] Military Strategy Research Department, PLA Academy of Military Science, 2013, p. 148.

[45] Military Strategy Research Department, PLA Academy of Military Scienceo, 2013, p. 145.

[46] Xu Qi, *On Military-Civilian Compatible Support System* [军民兼容保障系统论], Beijing: National Defense University Press [国防大学出版社], 2001.

[47] "Exploiting the Deterrence Effect of Military-Civilian Deep Fusion [发挥军民深度融合的威慑效应]," China Military Net [中国军网], April 28, 2015.

seem the ability to mobilize civilian resources to fight a sustained war could also make an important contribution to strategic deterrence.[48]

On the whole, judging the actual contribution of mobilization capacity and "military-civil fusion" to China's overall integrated strategic-deterrence posture appears to be much less straightforward than evaluating the contribution of its nuclear, conventional, space, and cyber-warfare capabilities. What is much clearer, however, is that Chinese military strategists see these as additional means of displaying China's growing military strength in ways that could influence a potential adversary's decisionmaking calculus and deter a would-be enemy from using force or the threat of force to challenge Chinese interests.

---

[48] The authors would like to thank Phillip Saunders for raising this important point about the deterrence effects of mobilization.

CHAPTER FOUR

Strategic-Deterrence Activities in Peacetime, Crisis, and War

Chinese military publications discuss a number of actions that can contribute to strategic deterrence in a general sense in peacetime, as well as more immediately in a crisis or conflict scenario.[1] According to SMS 2013, in peacetime, the PLA adopts "preventive deterrence activities" that correspond to the sources of potential threats to China's national security.[2] Specifically, when the threat of war is not immediate, a "peacetime deterrence posture" that is based on China's comprehensive national power and in particular its strategic capabilities "plays a role of maintaining a balanced relationship with the opponent for a relatively long period of time." This requires a "static deterrence capability."[3]

As strategic circumstances develop, however, China can adjust the "modes and intensities" of its actions to form a deterrence posture that helps ensure an opponent will not "dare to act lightly or rashly" against China's interests.[4] According to SMS 2013, when facing the threat of war or other urgent military security threats, China would

---

[1] The distinction adopted in SMS 2013 is at least somewhat reminiscent of the way in which Patrick Morgan distinguishes between "general" and "immediate" deterrence. On this distinction, see Patrick M. Morgan, *Deterrence: A Conceptual Analysis*, Beverly Hills, Calif.: Sage Publications, 1977.

[2] Military Strategy Research Department, PLA Academy of Military Science, 2013, p. 119.

[3] Military Strategy Research Department, PLA Academy of Military Science, 2013, p. 136.

[4] Military Strategy Research Department, PLA Academy of Military Science, 2013, p. 119.

need to shift to an "emergency deterrence posture" that poses a more-immediate threat to the opponent.[5] This would rely on "a dynamic deterrence capability,"[6] one that "takes applying military strength fully as the main body and draws support from other strengths as backing."[7] Moreover, in such a major military-crisis situation, the PLA can

> combine strategic unfolding with actual combat disposition to create a high intensity deterrence posture, to show strong resolve and willingness to fight and powerful actual strength, in order to force an adversary to promptly reverse course at the last minute before danger.[8]

PLA publications indicate that Chinese military forces—particularly PLASAF,[9] which controls China's strategic missile units—can use a variety of methods to carry out peacetime or crisis deterrence activities.[10] One such method is "exerting pressure through public opinion," which involves using print, broadcast, and electronic media to communicate information about the capabilities and deter-

---

[5]   Military Strategy Research Department, PLA Academy of Military Science, 2013, p. 136.

[6]   Although this approach shares the same name as Japan's "dynamic deterrence" concept, the two are very different. Japan's "dynamic deterrence" concept is intended to address what Japanese scholars and officials refer to as "gray zone" threats, such as Chinese attempts to undermine Japanese administrative control of the Senkaku Islands, which Beijing claims and refers to as the Diaoyu Islands. Japanese strategists highlight the difference between deterring challenges such as these and deterring more-traditional military threats such as a large-scale conventional attack or invasion. See, for example, Sugio Takahashi, "Crafting Deterrence and Defense: The New Defense Policy of Japan," The Tokyo Foundation, October 10, 2012.

[7]   Military Strategy Research Department, PLA Academy of Military Science, 2013, p. 136.

[8]   Military Strategy Research Department, PLA Academy of Military Science, 2013, p. 119. These deterrence actions should also help position the PLA to ensure a smooth transition from deterrence to combat operations if needed.

[9]   On December 31, 2015, PLASAF became the PLA Rocket Force as part of a major reorganization of China's military. This report, however, uses PLASAF to refer to China's strategic missile force for the most part, as it refers to sources published prior to the changes announced in January 2016. An exception is the portion of the report that discusses the reorganization, in which we use PLA Rocket Force to refer to what was previously PLASAF.

[10]   Li Xianyun et al., 2004, pp. 281–296; see also Zhao, 2005, p. 34.

mination of China's missile force to an enemy. The missile force can disseminate such information through a wide variety of channels, including television broadcasts, speeches, interviews with reporters, magazines and newspapers, and the Internet. For example, PLA publications indicate that military parades offer an excellent opportunity for China to display its strategic capabilities. Indeed, China's elaborate September 2015 military parade—the highlight of a series of events the CCP leadership held to mark the 70th anniversary of the end of World War II—allowed Beijing to showcase some of the PLA's newest advanced weapons. Among them were several types of China's newest and most advanced ballistic missiles, including DF-5B silo-based ICBMs,[11] which are capable of carrying MIRVs; DF-31A road-mobile ICBMs; DF-21D anti-ship ballistic missiles; and DF-26 intermediate-range ballistic missiles, which Chinese commentators said have nuclear, conventional, and anti-ship variants.[12] Similarly, PLASAF participated in a military parade on October 1, 2009, celebrating the 60th anniversary of the founding of the PRC; the event allowed Beijing to show off a number of key pieces of equipment, including DF-15 short-range ballistic missiles[13] and DF-31 road-mobile ICBMs.[14] The desired effect of such displays in peacetime is to bolster strategic deterrence in a general sense by highlighting improvements in China's military capabilities.[15] Some other specific methods that can be used include issuing statements about the development or deployment of new types of missiles

---

[11] Although China displayed its silo-based DF-5B ICBMs during the parade, it should be noted that, unlike the various types of mobile missiles that were carried by transporter erector launchers (TELs), the DF-5Bs were divided into two parts and carried on separate trailers. Additionally, these trailers did not have the erector capability needed to launch a missile.

[12] Andrew S. Erickson, "Missile March: China Parade Projects Patriotism at Home, Aims for Awe Abroad," *Wall Street Journal*, September 3, 2015.

[13] "DF-15B Ground Conventional Missile Unit [东风15B地地常规导弹方队]," People.cn [人民网], October 1, 2009.

[14] "National Day Grand Military Parade: DongFeng Shows Off Military Might [国庆大阅兵：东风壮军威]," *China Daily* [中国日报], October 10, 2009.

[15] In contrast, in a crisis or wartime, higher-intensity deterrence actions could be intended to produce a sense of "psychological shock" within the enemy leadership. See Li Xianyun et al., 2004, p. 282.

and releasing pictures or videos of missile-force exercises to the media. Although these examples focus on missile-force units, other parts of the PLA can also use television news broadcasts, press conferences, and the Internet to send deterrence messages. The commissioning of the aircraft carrier *Liaoning*, for instance, was done in an extremely high-profile way to highlight China's growing maritime capabilities and ambitions to both its neighbors and the world at large.[16]

PLA publications indicate that one of the most important campaign deterrence methods, particularly for the missile force, is making displays of strength. This mainly involves revealing missiles and various types of launch and support equipment and demonstrating the high-quality missile force personnel. There are numerous ways to demonstrate strength. Official Chinese military publications note that National Day parades often provide an opportunity for major powers to display their military strength; for nuclear powers, such parades provide an excellent opportunity to show off the strength of their nuclear missile forces, but China can display a wide range of nuclear and conventional military capabilities during such parades. Another way to demonstrate strength is to invite defense attachés, foreign military officers, and reporters to visit military facilities. In addition, PLA publications note that China can also deliberately reveal military activities, troop movements, and other strategic activities when enemy ISR satellites or planes are passing overhead or nearby. In some cases, however, it could be unclear what message, if any, such displays are intended to send, and observers could interpret them in a number of different ways.[17]

---

[16] "Our Nation's First Aircraft Carrier Officially Transferred to Navy, Hu Jintao Attends Commissioning Ceremony and Conducts Onboard Inspection, Wen Jiabao Reads Congratulatory Messages from Central Committee, State Council, Central Military Commission, Guo Boxiong, Xu Caihou, Ma Kai, Chang Wanquan, Wu Shengli Attend [我国第一艘航空母舰正式交付海军 胡锦涛出席交接入列仪式并登舰视察 温家宝宣读党中央国务院中央军委贺电 郭伯雄徐才厚马凯常万全吴胜利出席]," *PLA Daily* [解放军报], September 26, 2012.

[17] For example, in late May 2015, China reportedly placed mobile artillery weapons systems on one of its reclaimed islands in the South China Sea. "Asian military attachés and analysts said the placement of mobile artillery pieces appeared to be a symbol of intent," suggesting they believed this was a deliberate decision by Chinese leaders to leak this information as a

Chinese testing of developmental weapon systems—and official confirmation of some tests—also may be intended to bolster strategic deterrence in peacetime. For example, one Chinese commentator, He Qisong of the Shanghai University of Political Science and Law, suggested that China's June 2015 hypersonic-glide vehicle flight test was likely intended to contribute to nuclear deterrence by demonstrating China's ability to field a capability designed to penetrate missile-defense systems.[18] Another example is provided by China's testing of its own missile-defense capabilities. PLA publications have stressed the deterrence effects of missile defense—not simply by displaying improvements in Chinese technology but also by showing the PLA's ability to match or potentially exceed the results achieved by other major powers. For instance, a 2012 article in the academic journal of the National University of Defense Technology notes the extensive investments that the United States, Russia, India, and Japan have made to their missile-defense systems and argues that China should do the same. The article argues that this system could act as a deterrent to real threats in the surrounding environment and provide effective support to limited nuclear deterrent forces, thereby influencing the enemy's decisionmaking. Overall, the article argues that developing the national missile-defense system can protect national security, seize a strategically advantageous position, provide an important means of support, lead technological innovation, contribute to the development of industry, and continue to drive economic growth.[19] As with some other means of deterrence signaling, however, it is possible that weapons tests intended principally to meet program-development requirements or to bolster deterrence in a general sense could be misinterpreted as a more specifically directed strategic message even if none is intended.

---

warning to anyone who would challenge China's claims of sovereignty. Raju Gopalakrishnan, "U.S. Says China Has Placed Mobile Artillery on Reclaimed Island," *Reuters*, May 29, 2015.

[18] Keck, 2015.

[19] Shen Di and Hou Guanghua [沈堤, 侯广华], "The Development of Our Nation's Ballistic Missile Defense System Should Insist on the 'Four Establishes' [我国弹道导弹防御系统发展应坚持'四个确立'], "*National Defense Technology* [国防科技], 2012.

Other methods of conducting strategic-deterrence operations that are described in Chinese missile force publications would likely be more relevant in a crisis or conflict situation, in line with the discussion of an "emergency deterrence posture" that appears in SMS 2013. One of these is "raising the level of weapons preparation." This entails increasing the level of readiness of the missile force in accordance with the appropriate regulations on levels of weapons preparation. The purpose is to demonstrate different degrees of deterrence strength and preparation. Throughout the process of increasing the level of weapons preparation, missile-force officers must be careful about what they reveal to the enemy. They must reveal enough information about their preparations to deter the enemy, but they must conceal information that could expose vulnerabilities. According to *Science of Second Artillery Campaigns* (SSAC), an internal document published by the PLASAF to guide its members in their thinking about missile-force development and operations, because the technical preparation of missiles is usually carried out in central storage facilities under conditions of concealment, the enemy is unlikely to detect the increased readiness of Chinese missile systems. Consequently, the missile force must record videos of the preparations and distribute them via television and the Internet, but the scenes that are revealed must be carefully selected in order to avoid divulging technical secrets.

Another related concept is "using the troops to build momentum." According to SSAC, this concept of building momentum refers to using troop deployments to create an advantageous situation for China, in part by confusing the enemy about China's operational intentions. Methods identified in SSAC include maneuvering troops, combining real and feint maneuvers, conducting simulated missile launches, electronic feints, and "all-out escalation."[20] Maneuvering troops involves moving missile launchers and support vehicles as the enemy's reconnaissance satellites are about to pass overhead. The purpose is to place psychological pressure on enemy decisionmakers and deter them from engaging in potentially risky actions by showing them that China's missile forces are preparing to conduct combat operations.

---

[20] Li Xianyun et al., 2004, pp. 288–290.

Combining real and feint maneuvers creates an advantageous situation by using a small number of actual combat troops in combination with forces equipped with fake missiles and equipment that are engaging in feint activities. This creates the impression that a larger number of forces are involved in the maneuvers, which in turn is supposed to increase the overall effects of the deterrence operations.

Chinese missile-force units can also attempt to create momentum by conducting simulated missile launches. For China's solid-fueled mobile systems, this involves deploying the mobile missile forces to training areas and fake launch sites just before the enemy's reconnaissance satellites are about to pass overhead. The mobile missile units can then prepare their equipment, erect the missiles, and conduct pre-launch inspections. China's liquid-fueled missiles can "carry out simulated fueling."[21] Whichever missiles are used, the purpose is to persuade the enemy to believe that China's missile forces are prepared to strike enemy targets, thus convincing the enemy to abandon or refrain from actions that China considers particularly threatening. This approach could blur the line between deterrence and coercion, depending on the specifics of the scenario. According to SSAC, simulated missile launches

> make the enemy believe that our missile forces are already in a situation of waiting for an opportunity or conducting pre-combat exercises; because of this, the enemy will consider the consequences and abandon some of its activities.[22]

Electronic feint is a deception technique that involves the use of electronic equipment and communications gear to simulate the electromagnetic radiation characteristics and communications patterns of missile-force and command-center activities. The purpose is to confuse the enemy intelligence personnel and decisionmakers so that they will reach inaccurate conclusions about the missile force's real activities.

---

[21] Li Xianyun et al, 2004, p. 289.

[22] Li Xianyun et al, 2004, p. 289.

Their inability to determine what is really going on will worry them and deter them from taking action.

The "all-out escalation" option involves ordering silo-based missiles and missile units at launch pads to conduct technical preparations of missile weaponry at the same time. This approach involves using many types of media to transmit recordings of these operational preparations to foreign audiences. The intent is to ensure that the enemy sees that the missile force is reaching a heightened state of preparedness. This is intended to create enough fear in the minds of the enemy decisionmakers to cause them to reconsider the potential consequences of their actions and refrain from taking steps that could result in Chinese retaliation.[23]

Conducting launch exercises is another important method to achieve campaign deterrence objectives. This tactic involves launching missiles at predetermined ground or sea targets to place psychological pressure on enemy decisionmakers. SSAC characterizes launch exercises as mid- or high-strength deterrence activities in relation to how close they come to actual combat. In addition to creating psychological pressure or even panic on the enemy side and producing the desired deterrence effects, launch exercises have the added benefit of testing the operational capabilities of missile-force units because they involve firing real missiles.

Another option is test-launching missiles close to enemy territory or enemy ships. The objective of this tactic is to convince the enemy that provoking China may risk a devastating missile attack. This is considered a high-strength deterrence option. For example, one option is conducting "test launches from both flanks," which requires launching missiles at two or more important enemy targets. Another is a "cross-island offensive test launch," which involves launching a missile across an enemy-held island.

---

[23] Li Xianyun et al., 2004, pp. 289–290.

Yet another option is launching one or more missiles close to an enemy aircraft carrier. According to SSAC,

> when conducting deterrence strikes against an enemy aircraft carrier battle group that is intruding into our territorial waters, we can launch missiles near their flanks or in front of them to demonstrate that we have the capability and determination to carry out a destructive strike against the enemy's nuclear-powered carrier; this will frighten the enemy into leaving our territorial waters.[24]

The final campaign deterrence method discussed in SSAC is "lowering the nuclear deterrence threshold" or "adjusting nuclear policy." The authors suggest that China could drop or place conditions on its longstanding no-first-use policy in response to particularly threatening conventional attacks by a powerful enemy. Specifically, they state that this method could be used when a powerful nuclear-armed enemy that enjoys conventional military superiority conducts continuous medium- or high-intensity air raids against major strategic targets in China. Under such circumstances, the "Supreme Command"[25] could choose to "adjust" China's longstanding no-first-use nuclear deterrence policy and order the missile force to "actively carry out powerful nuclear deterrence against the enemy to deter the enemy from continuously launching conventional air raids against [China's] major strategic targets."[26]

The authors of SSAC highlight four conditions under which the Supreme Command might "reduce the nuclear deterrence threshold" to deter an enemy from conducting conventional strategic attacks; three of the four cover conventional strategic attacks against China. The first is when the enemy threatens to carry out conventional strikes

---

[24] Li Xianyun et al., 2004, pp. 292–293.

[25] Chinese military publications sometimes use the term *Supreme Command* [*zuigao tongshuaibu*] to refer to the highest-level members of the CCP and military decisionmakers. PLA publications such as SSAC appear to indicate it is the body that would make all of the key strategic-level decisions, but they do not specify its exact membership or fully enumerate its responsibilities.

[26] Li Xianyun et al., 2004, p. 294.

against China's nuclear facilities or nuclear power stations; the second is when an enemy threatens to carry out attacks against major strategic targets such as hydroelectric power stations; the third is when an enemy threatens to carry out attacks against the capital, major cities, or other political or economic centers. In all three cases, the purpose of adjusting China's nuclear policy and issuing nuclear threats in response to conventional air attacks would be to frighten the enemy into stopping (or at least reducing) the strength of its conventional air strikes. The fourth case in which China might consider "lowering the nuclear deterrence threshold" arises when China is facing serious danger or impending disaster because it is losing a conventional military conflict in which the stakes are very high. According to SSAC, when a conventional conflict is continuing to escalate and the overall strategic situation is becoming extremely disadvantageous for China, national safety and survival may be seriously threatened. In such a situation, the Supreme Command could adjust China's nuclear policy and order nuclear missile-force units to carry out effective deterrence against the enemy. If the threat the enemy presents is severe enough China can increase the pressure on enemy leaders even further by revealing the aim points of its nuclear weapons. Disclosing the potential targets of nuclear strikes represents the "highest level of deterrence," according to SSAC.

Chinese military publications also highlight the importance of space deterrence in crisis or conflict situations. According to one publication, for example,

> in future military conflicts, all kinds of threats may be used against enemy space capabilities, using them as hostages and collateral and causing them not to dare to adopt hostile action. This will be particularly true [in conflicts] against advanced nations whose reliance on space is particularly high.[27]

---

[27] Yang Xuejun, Zhang Wangxin, Shui Jing, Wang Tianzhong, Ren Dexin, Zou Hanbing, Wu Min, and Guo Ping, *Advantage Comes From Space: The Space Battlefield and Space Operations* [优势来自空间－论空间战场与空间作战], Beijing: Guofang gongye chubanshe, 2006, pp. 90–91.

In such situations, the media may herald technological advances in military space capabilities, or the PLA may conduct space launches or exercises to demonstrate its space power and produce powerful deterrence effects.[28]

Finally, Chinese military publications indicate that limited military action—such as small-scale air and missile strikes or computer network attacks—can also be employed as a form of strategic deterrence, suggesting that the PLA might employ limited amounts of force for demonstration purposes, perhaps to compel a rival to accept Beijing's demands or to deter a potential adversary from intervening in a conflict involving China. For example, according to SMS 2013, PLA strategic-deterrence operations can also include "activities that border on warfare," such a "limited but effective firepower strikes of a warning nature and information attacks."[29]

---

[28] Yang et al., 2006, pp. 90–91.

[29] Military Strategy Research Department, PLA Academy of Military Science, 2013, p. 119.

CHAPTER FIVE

Implications and Conclusions

For China, integrated strategic deterrence appears to be more than a means of demonstrating that diverse capabilities operated by different parts of the PLA all contribute to the strategic-deterrence mission. Indeed, integrated strategic deterrence is a concept that is likely to have important operational implications. Moreover, China's development of an increasingly sophisticated suite of strategic capabilities is giving China the integrated strategic deterrence posture the PLA has outlined in several publications, beginning with the chapter on strategic deterrence that appeared in SMS 2001 and continuing through SMS 2013. Now that Chinese capabilities are catching up with these concepts, analysts of Chinese military affairs should expect to see the PLA increasingly displaying them for strategic-deterrence purposes as outlined in a number of Chinese military publications. For general peacetime strategic-deterrence purposes, this could include actions such as demonstrating new capabilities through weapons tests, displaying them during military parades, incorporating them into training and exercises, and revealing them to international observers through official media, unofficial Internet postings, and other channels. In a crisis or conflict, the PLA could adopt a much-higher intensity—and potentially highly escalatory—approach to deterrence operations, such as by increasing the readiness level of its strategic forces; displaying its nuclear, long-range conventional strike or anti-satellite weapons to send a deterrence signal; conducting nuclear or conventional missile test launches; or even conducting limited conventional or non-kinetic strikes designed to deter further escalation or compel an adversary to cease actions China perceives as extremely threatening.

As a result of these developments, China's growing capabilities could have important implications. The remainder of this section addresses the potential implications for Chinese policy and strategy; strategic stability and escalation management; and U.S. extended deterrence and assurance of allies.

Implications for China's Approach to Deterrence Policy and Strategy

Chinese thinking about strategic deterrence appears to be evolving as China revises its perceptions of its external security environment and improves its military capabilities. First, China's assessment of its external security environment may motivate changes in its thinking about the requirements of integrated strategic deterrence. PLA strategists appear to regard the U.S. rebalance to Asia as part of what they often characterize as a broader pattern of U.S. attempts to "contain" China's growing power and influence. These strategists are concerned about the possibility that improvements in U.S. capabilities—particularly in the areas of missile defense, intelligence, surveillance, and reconnaissance, and conventional prompt global-strike capabilities—could undermine the deterrent credibility of China's strategic missile force. Additionally, other actors could begin to figure more prominently in China's strategic-deterrence calculations in the future. China currently sees the United States as its main potential adversary in determining its nuclear force structure and other strategic-deterrence requirements. It is possible, however, that China could become more concerned about the nuclear capabilities of India, which could result in changes such as a larger arsenal of theater nuclear missiles. Indeed, China could consider adopting a different approach to deal with India as a nuclear rival, one that could diverge from China's longstanding focus on deploying a secure second-strike capability without matching the numbers of weapons in the arsenals of the nuclear superpowers. Whereas China accepts an asymmetric nuclear relationship with the United States and

Russia, so long as it can maintain a secure second-strike capability, it could very well choose a different approach to dealing with India. For example, if India increased the size of its nuclear forces to a level that rivaled China's, Beijing might feel a need to build a larger arsenal than India's. China may do this even if only because it judged that, for reasons of status, it must avoid the perception—whether domestically or internationally—that the two countries are on an equal footing as far as military power is concerned. This concern about avoiding the appearance of failing to stay ahead of India's military technology developments could also influence China's thinking about its requirements for the deployment of strategic missile-defense capabilities.[1]

Second, China's growing nuclear deterrence, conventional precision strike, space and counter-space, and network-warfare capabilities will create some new options for Chinese strategists and decisionmakers, which will probably lead to debates about many aspects of China's approach to strategic deterrence. At the very least, as the PLA continues to deploy new and improved capabilities, this will present Chinese leaders with a wider ranger of policy and strategy options, and it could even lead to changes in longstanding aspects of Chinese policy and strategy. For example, at least one important PLA publication, the 2013 edition of the SMS, has raised the possibility that, as the PLA's strategic early-warning capabilities improve, China may want to adopt a launch-under-attack or launch-on-warning posture for its nuclear missile force, an option the authors suggest would strengthen deterrence without violating China's nuclear no-first-use policy. They write:

> When conditions are met, and when necessary, one can rapidly launch a nuclear missile counterstrike when it has been clearly determined that the enemy has already launched nuclear missiles against us but said enemy nuclear warheads have yet to arrive at their targets and effectively explode or cause actual damage to us. This both conforms to our country's consistent policy of no first use of nuclear weapons and also effectively prevents our nuclear

---

[1] See Bruce W. McDonald and Charles D. Ferguson, *Understanding the Dragon Shield: Likelihood and Implications of Chinese Strategic Ballistic Missile Defense*, Federation of American Scientists, September 2015.

forces from suffering greater losses, improving the survivability of nuclear missile forces and their counterstrike capabilities.[2]

Disturbingly, however, the book that raises this possibility does not address any of the risks associated with this approach.[3] This raises questions about the extent to which Chinese strategists have considered the risks associated with new options, such as the escalation risks and other problems that might be associated with such a posture should China decide to pursue one when permitted by improvements in its early-warning capabilities.

Still another factor that could become more important in shaping China's strategic-deterrence concepts and capabilities is competition for resources and rivalry between parts of the PLA that appear determined to maintain—or, in some cases, expand—their role in the strategic deterrence–mission area. In November 2015, China announced plans for a major reorganization of the PLA's command structure, and on December 31, 2015, it began to implement these changes with the establishment of a separate headquarters for the PLA ground force, the transformation of PLASAF into PLA Rocket Force, and the formation of a new PLA Strategic Support Force. It is as yet unclear, however, how this will influence the potential for bureaucratic competition in this area among different components of the PLA, such as a struggle between the PLAAF and China's missile force over space and counterspace capabilities that appears to have emerged in recent years. Finally, it remains unclear exactly how some of the disparate elements of integrated strategic deterrence relate to one another in the view of Chinese strategists, suggesting that analysts should be alert to the possibility of

---

[2]   Military Strategy Research Department, PLA Academy of Military Science, 2013.

[3]   Indeed, as Gregory Kulacki has pointed out, "There is no discussion of the strategic challenges associated with a decision to launch on warning, particularly the risk of an accidental or erroneous launch either due to false or ambiguous warning, technical problems or damage to the early warning systems, or poor judgment." See Gregory Kulacki, "The Chinese Military Updates China's Nuclear Strategy," Cambridge, Mass.: Union of Concerned Scientists, March 2015, p. 4.

further developments in Chinese thinking as it relates to the issue of linkages between different types of strategic-deterrence capabilities.[4]

Escalation Management Challenges

China's integrated strategic deterrence concepts and capabilities create several possible escalation risks. One challenge for escalation management derives from organizational issues, specifically the diffusion of various parts of China's integrated strategic deterrence posture across multiple components of the PLA and the absence of an entity such as United States Strategic Command (USSTRATCOM) to integrate and coordinate the employment of these capabilities. In particular, this could be problematic for strategic signaling purposes. One possibility is for China to coordinate and de-conflict the different aspects of its integrated strategic deterrence at the level of the Central Military Commission, China's highest level of military leadership.

Another possibility is to give the leading role to China's strategic missile force, the PLA Rocket Force (previously known as PLASAF), which could carry out this function under the direct command of the Central Military Commission and the leadership of the CCP. China's strategic missile force controls the majority of China's nuclear weapons and its most potent long-range conventional strike capabilities, and it appears poised to play a central role in counter-space operations and "space deterrence." China describes the PLA Rocket Force as China's "core force for strategic deterrence,"[5] as it did PLASAF prior to the January 2016 reorganization. As the PLA Rocket Force continues to

---

[4] For example, the sources reviewed for this report highlight the complementarity of different types of strategic-deterrence capabilities. They note that some cover areas that others do not, such as conventional forces being useful to deter threats that do not rise to a level of severity that would make nuclear weapons a credible response, but they do not clearly explain Chinese views on other important issues. For instance, they do not address considerations such as how weaknesses or vulnerabilities in one domain might be offset by advantages in another or exactly how capabilities in one domain could be used to deter (or perhaps to inadvertently trigger) escalation in another domain.

[5] See, for example, "New Branch of PLA Shows Off Missiles in Music Video," *Global Times*, February 14, 2016.

develop its nuclear, conventional, space, and perhaps information warfare capabilities, it could increasingly be considered a powerful integrated strategic deterrence force in its own right. For example, SMS 2013 highlights the missile force's role in enabling the PLA to expand its operations into other domains, most notably space. The book suggests that China's strategic missile force will focus on "developing new types of operations methods" and will thus play an increasingly important role in the space and information domains.[6]

The problem of ambiguity arises regarding whether a particular deterrence action is a nuclear or conventional signal because the PLA Rocket Force controls both nuclear and conventional ballistic missiles. Moreover, several other parts of the PLA spread across multiple services control other integrated strategic deterrence capabilities. Beyond the PLA Rocket Force, these include, at a minimum, PLAN, PLAAF, and PLA Strategic Support Force. As for nuclear weapons, PLA Rocket Force and PLAN currently control nuclear capabilities, and PLAAF may join them if it deploys dual-capable bombers armed with nuclear weapons in the future. PLA Rocket Force, PLAN, and PLAAF all control important capabilities that contribute to conventional deterrence. As for space and cyberspace, prior to the January 2016 reorganization, PLAAF and PLASAF appeared to be contending for influence in military space and counter-space, an area in which the General Staff Department and the General Armaments Department also played important roles. Similarly, multiple components of the PLA either play a role in cyber operations or may aspire to do so. This raises questions about how China would think about actually integrating disparate

---

[6] With respect to space, this is in part because PLASAF's missile capabilities could be modified to carry out spacecraft launches. It is also as a result of the development of ground-based missiles capable of carrying out attacks against satellites. Specifically, according to page 233 of SMS 2013,

> The expansion of national security interests and development and transformation of the pattern of warfare, are making struggles and confrontations that utilize the fields of space and the Internet more and more intense, and this raises new requirements for military capability development. Having a foothold in and relying on the special points and advantages of guided missile weaponry, developing new types of operations methods, and taking PLASAF operations capabilities into space and other new domains of development, are important directions in PLASAF construction and development.

instruments of strategic deterrence, given that these different parts of the PLA control capabilities such as silo-based and road-mobile ICBMs and long-range conventional missiles; nuclear-powered ballistic missile submarines; ASAT weapons; and information- and electronic- warfare capabilities. Indeed, this diffusion of strategic-deterrence capabilities across multiple parts of the PLA may make truly integrated employment of these capabilities for signaling purposes challenging and therefore make managing escalation as envisioned in PLA publications much more difficult in practice than in theory.

Additionally, the PLA organizational reforms China is currently implementing could have important implications for China's ability to coordinate and employ its strategic-deterrence capabilities, but it is as yet unclear whether this will make it easier or harder for China to manage escalation risks in a crisis or conflict scenario. Carrying out a major reorganization of the PLA's command structure is a high priority for Xi Jinping, as reflected by the November 2013 Communiqué of the Third Plenum of the 18th Central Committee, which highlighted the importance of

> deepening the adjustment and reform of the military administrative setup and staffing, promoting adjustment and reform of military policies and systems, and deepening the integration between the military and civilian sectors.[7]

This announcement and the subsequent establishment of the Leading Group for Deepening of National Defense and Military Reform make it very clear that China intends to fully implement a major reorganization of the PLA, and this is already playing out with the above-mentioned changes put into effect in January 2016.[8] It remains to be seen, however, exactly how the organizational reforms will play out and what influence they will have in terms of China's ability to manage

---

[7] "Communiqué of the Third Plenary Session of the 18th Central Committee of the Communist Party of China," china.org, November 12, 2013.

[8] See James Mulvenon, "Groupthink? PLA Leading Small Groups and the Prospect for Real Reform and Change in the Chinese Military," *China Leadership Monitor*, No. 44, July 28, 2014.

and coordinate its growing strategic-deterrence capabilities, but the new command and control mechanism called for in the November 2013 Third Plenum Communiqué and subsequent statements about PLA organizational reform is clearly a potential means to address these coordination challenges.

Implications for Extended Deterrence and Assurance of U.S. Allies

China's integrated strategic deterrence concepts and capabilities will also have implications for U.S. extended deterrence and assurance of allies and partners in the region. Allies and regional partners will be concerned not only about the possibility they will become targets of Chinese threats in some or all of the relevant domains, but also that China could wield its growing capabilities in ways that are intended to undermine U.S. willingness or ability to intervene militarily to support its allies in the event of a crisis or conflict in the region.[9] As China improves and attempts to coordinate its nuclear, conventional, space, and network warfare capabilities in pursuit of an integrated strategic deterrent, China's advances in these areas are likely to become a growing concern for U.S. regional allies and partners. Accordingly, all of these areas will need to be fully incorporated into U.S. discussions and exchanges with regional allies, including new efforts to work with allies on building a common understanding of the threat and developing multidimensional response options.

Conclusion

The PLA's ability to execute integrated strategic deterrence is catching up with the concept. In particular, the PLA's growing nuclear,

---

[9]   Interviews with Chinese analysts suggest they are concerned that the United States could attempt to wield its own capabilities in these areas to coerce China into accepting U.S. demands. These analysts view China's development of similar capabilities in the context of ensuring they will be able to deter or counter any such moves by the United States.

long-range conventional strike, space and counter-space, and cyber-warfare capabilities, along with China's focus on mobilization and "military-civil fusion," are strengthening China's strategic-deterrence posture and giving the PLA a menu of strategic-deterrence actions it can execute in the event of a regional crisis or conflict that could involve the United States. Future developments in this area are likely to include capabilities such as road-mobile ICBMs capable of carrying MIRVs to enhance the land-based component of China's nuclear deterrent force; more-advanced SSBNs and SLBMs to strengthen the emerging sea-based leg of China's nuclear deterrent; hypersonic-glide vehicles that could further enhance China's nuclear deterrent posture or perhaps give Beijing at least a limited conventional prompt global-strike capability; further improvements in the conventional long-range strike capabilities of Chinese air, naval, and missile forces; space and counter-space systems that could contribute to the strategic-deterrence mission, including space-based early warning systems and several types of kinetic and non-kinetic counter-space capabilities; and improved cyber- and electronic- warfare capabilities. Analysts should also expect to see Beijing employ at least some of these capabilities for strategic-deterrence purposes, even if only in a peacetime, general deterrence context. This could involve displaying them in military parades, demonstrating them in training or exercises, or unveiling them in other ways discussed in Chinese military publications, such as in official or unofficial media reports or by deliberately revealing them when other countries' satellites are passing overhead.

As China's strategic-deterrence capabilities continue to grow, analysts will need to watch carefully for signs that Chinese leaders are considering changes to policy and strategy that could be enabled by some of their new capabilities. In particular, observers will need to keep an eye out for potentially destabilizing moves, such as adoption of a launch-on-warning policy. China's growing strategic-deterrence capabilities may also require focused U.S. responses in a number of ways. The United States will need to invest in maintaining its own strategic-deterrence capabilities, enhance the survivability and resilience of its forces in the region, and reduce its dependence on space and information systems that are potentially vulnerable to disruption.

The United States will also need to work to build shared understanding by pursuing a broader U.S.-China dialogue on strategic-deterrence and stability issues. Finally, the United States will likely have to take an increasingly multidimensional approach to assuring its allies that it will continue to maintain the capability and the resolve to support them in a crisis, even as China further strengthens its integrated strategic deterrence capabilities.

References

"America's Cyberspace Strategy Shifting to 'Strategic Deterrence and Offensive Operations' [美国网络空间战略正向'战略威慑和进攻行动'转变]," *Study Times* [学习时报], June 15, 2015. As of October 13, 2015:
http://www.cac.gov.cn/2015-06/15/c_1115613673.htm

Blasko, Dennis J., "Military Parades Demonstrate Chinese Concept of Deterrence," *China Brief*, Vol. 9, No. 8, April 16, 2009. As of October 13, 2015:
http://www.jamestown.org/single/?tx_ttnews%5Btt_news%5D=34869&no_cache=1#.VWydKOsX-fQ

Chase, Michael S., "Defense and Deterrence in China's Military Space Strategy," *China Brief*, Vol. 11, No. 5, March 25, 2011. As of February 12, 2016:
http://www.jamestown.org/single/?no_cache=1&tx_ttnews%5Btt_news%5D=37699

———, "China's Transition to a More Credible Nuclear Deterrent: Implications and Challenges for the United States," *Asia Policy*, Vol. 16, 2013, pp. 69–101.

Chase, Michael S., Andrew Erickson, and Chris Yeaw, "Chinese Theater and Strategic Missile Force Modernization and Its Implications for the United States," *Journal of Strategic Studies*, Vol. 32, No. 1, 2009, pp. 67–114.

Cheng, Dean, "Chinese Views on Deterrence," *Joint Force Quarterly*, No. 60, 1st Quarter, 2011, pp. 92–94.

———, "The PLA's Interest in Space Dominance: Testimony Before U.S.-China Economic and Security Review Commission," Washington, D.C.: The Heritage Foundation, February 18, 2015. As of February 15, 2016:
http://www.uscc.gov/sites/default/files/Cheng_Testimony.pdf

"China's Military Strategy [中国的军事战略]," Ministry of National Defense of the People's Republic of China [中华人民共和国国防部], May 2015. As of October 13, 2015:
http://www.mod.gov.cn/affair/2015-05/26/content_4588132.htm

"China's National Defense in 2008," Information Office of the State Council, People's Republic of China, January 2009.

Chinese Military Encyclopedia, Supplemental Volume [中国军事百科全书, 增补], Beijing: Military Science Academy Press [军事科学出版社], November 2002.

Chinese Military Encyclopedia, Volume 3: Military Academia II [中国军事百科全书 3: 军事学术 II], Beijing: Military Science Academy Press [军事科学出版社], 1997.

Chinese Strategic Missile Force Encyclopedia [中国战略导弹部队百科全书], Beijing: Chinese Encyclopedia Press [中国百科全书出版社], May 2012.

"Communiqué of the Third Plenary Session of the 18th Central Committee of the Communist Party of China," China.org.cn, November 12, 2013. As of February 18, 2016:
http://www.china.org.cn/china/third_plenary_session/2014-01/15/content_31203056.htm

"DF-15B Ground Conventional Missile Unit [东风15B地地常规导弹方队]," People.cn [人民网], October 1, 2009. As of October 13, 2015:
http://military.people.com.cn/GB/8221/84385/134407/158575/10150702.html

DoD—*See* U.S. Department of Defense.

Erickson, Andrew S., "Missile March: China Parade Projects Patriotism at Home, Aims for Awe Abroad," *Wall Street Journal*, September 3, 2015. As of October 13, 2015:
http://blogs.wsj.com/chinarealtime/2015/09/03/missile-march-china-parade-projects-patriotism-at-home-aims-for-awe-abroad

"Exploiting the Deterrence Effect of Military-Civilian Deep Fusion [发挥军民深度融合的威慑效应]," China Military Net [中国军网], April 28, 2015. As of October 13, 2015:
http://military.people.com.cn/n/2015/0428/c172467-26914399.html

Fan Jishe [樊吉社], "The Effect of a National Missile Defense System on the Global Security Structure [国家导弹防御系统对全球战略格局的影响]," Chinese Academy of Social Sciences [中国社会科学院], March 15, 2001. As of October 13, 2015:
http://ias.cass.cn/show/show_project_ls.asp?id=273

Gong Ting [龚婷], ed., "Nuclear, Fifty Years in China [核，来到中国50年]," China Institute of International Studies [中国国际问题研究院], October 21, 2014. As of October 13, 2015:
http://www.ciis.org.cn/chinese/2014-10/21/content_7309871.htm

Gopalakrishnan, Raju, "U.S. Says China Has Placed Mobile Artillery on Reclaimed Island," Reuters, May 29, 2015. As of February 12, 2016:
http://www.reuters.com/article/2015/05/29/us-asia-security-island-idUSKBN0OE12T20150529

Hallion, Richard P., Roger Cliff, and Phillip C. Saunders, eds., *The Chinese Air Force: Evolving Concepts, Roles, and Capabilities*, Washington, D.C.: National Defense University, 2012.

Heginbotham, Eric, Michael Nixon, Forrest E. Morgan, Jacob Heim, Jeff Hagen, Sheng Li, Jeffrey Engstrom, Martin C. Libicki, Paul DeLuca, David A. Shlapak, David R. Frelinger, Burgess Laird, Kyle Brady, and Lyle J. Morris, *The U.S.-China Military Scorecard: Forces, Geography, and the Evolving Balance of Power, 1996–2017*, Santa Monica, Calif: RAND Corporation, RR-392-AF, 2015. As of February 17, 2016: http://www.rand.org/pubs/research_reports/RR392.html

Keck, Zachary, "Why America Should Fear China's Hypersonic Nuclear Missile," *The National Interest*, June 15, 2015. As of October 13, 2015: http://www.nationalinterest.org/blog/the-buzz/ why-america-should-fear-chinas-hypersonic-nuclear-missile-13115

Krepon, Michael, "China's Military Space Strategy: An Exchange," *Survival*, Vol. 50, No. 1, February–March 2008, pp. 157–198. As of February 12, 2016: http://www.tandfonline.com/doi/abs/10.1080/00396330801899512

Kulacki, Gregory, "The Chinese Military Updates China's Nuclear Strategy," Cambridge, Mass.: Union of Concerned Scientists, March 2015. As of October 13, 2015: http://www.ucsusa.org/sites/default/files/attach/2015/03/chinese-nuclear-strategy-full-report.pdf

Lewis, Jeffrey, "China's Nuclear Modernization: Surprise, Restraint, and Uncertainty," in Ashley J. Tellis, Abraham M. Denmark, and Travis Tanner, eds., *Strategic Asia 2013–14: Asia in the Second Nuclear Age*, Seattle, Wash.: National Bureau of Asian Research, October 2013, pp. 67–96.

Li Bin, "China's Nuclear Strategy," presentation at Carnegie International Nonproliferation Conference, Washington, D.C., June 25–26, 2007. As of February 15, 2016: http://carnegieendowment.org/files/deter_disarm_li.pdf

———, "What China's Missile Intercept Test Means," Carnegie Endowment for International Peace, February 4, 2013. As of October 13, 2015: http://carnegieendowment.org/2013/02/04/what-china-s-missile-intercept-test-means/ fa45

Li Li [李莉], "A New Space for Strategic Competition [战略博弈新空间]," World Knowledge [世界知识], 2011.

Li Xianyun [李贤允], Rong Jiaxin [容嘉信], Shao Yuanming [邵元明], Ge Xinqing [葛信卿], Huang Zongyuan [黄宗元], Wang Zengyong [王增勇], Chang Jin'an [常金安], Lü Xiangdong, [吕向东], Wang Xiaodong [王晓东], Huang Wei [黄伟], Mao Guanghong [毛光宏], Zhou Min [周敏], Wu Min [武旻], Chen Changming [陈昌明], Li Chaomin [李朝民], *Science of Second Artillery Campaigns* [第二炮兵战役学], Yu Jixun [于际训] and Li Tilin [李体林], eds., Beijing: PLA Press [解放军出版社], March 2004.

Liang Yabin [梁亚滨], "Network Space Is the New Domain for National Competition in the Big Data Era [网络空间是大数据时代国家博弈的新领域]," *Study Times* [学习时报], October 20, 2014. As of October 13, 2015: http://theory.people.com.cn/n/2014/1020/c40531-25866183.html

McDonald, Bruce W., and Charles D. Ferguson, *Understanding the Dragon Shield: Likelihood and Implications of Chinese Strategic Ballistic Missile Defense, Federation of American Scientists*, September 2015.

McReynolds, Joe, "China's Evolving Perspectives on Network Warfare: Lessons from the Science of Military Strategy," *China Brief*, Vol. 15, No. 8, April 16, 2015. As of February 12, 2016: http://www.jamestown.org/programs/chinabrief/single/?tx_ttnews%5Bttnews%5D=43798&tx_ttnews%5BbackPid%5D=25&cHash=dfc1ff0f1f7bda6c3b54a7f244b8376b#.Vr6PgHQrIsO

Military Strategy Research Department, PLA Academy of Military Science, *The Science of Military Strategy* [战略学], 3rd ed., Beijing: Military Science Press [军事科学出版社], 2013.

Morgan, Patrick M., *Deterrence: A Conceptual Analysis*, Beverly Hills, Calif.: Sage Publications, 1977.

Mulvenon, James, "Groupthink? PLA Leading Small Groups and the Prospect for Real Reform and Change in the Chinese Military," *China Leadership Monitor*, No. 44, July 28, 2014. As of October 13, 2015: http://www.hoover.org/sites/default/files/research/docs/clm44jm.pdf

———, "PLA Computer Network Operations: Scenarios, Doctrine, Organizations, and Capability," in Roy Kamphausen, David Lai, and Andrew Scobell, eds., *Beyond the Strait: PLA Missions Other than Taiwan*, Carlisle, Pa.: U.S. Army War College, Strategic Studies Institute, April 2009. As of October 13, 2015: http://www.strategicstudiesinstitute.army.mil/pubs/display.cfm?pubID=910

"National Day Grand Military Parade: DongFeng Shows Off Military Might [国庆大阅兵: 东风壮军威]," *China Daily* [中国日报], October 10, 2009. As of October 13, 2015: http://www.chinadaily.com.cn/dfpd/2009-10/10/content_9157744.htm

"National Defense White Paper: Diversified Uses of China's Military Forces [国防白皮书：中国武装力量的多样化运用]," Ministry of National Defense of the People's Republic of China [中华人民共和国国防部], April 2013. As of October 13, 2015:
http://www.mod.gov.cn/affair/2013-04/16/content_4442839.htm

"New Branch of PLA Shows Off Missiles in Music Video," *Global Times*, February 14, 2016. As of March 10, 2016:
http://www.globaltimes.cn/content/968296.shtml

"Our Nation's First Aircraft Carrier Officially Transferred to Navy, Hu Jintao Attends Commissioning Ceremony and Conducts Onboard Inspection, Wen Jiabao Reads Congratulatory Messages from Central Committee, State Council, Central Military Commission, Guo Boxiong, Xu Caihou, Ma Kai, Chang Wanquan, Wu Shengli Attend [我国第一艘航空母舰正式交付海军 胡锦涛出席交接入列仪式并登舰视察 温家宝宣读党中央国务院中央军委贺电 郭伯雄徐才厚马凯常万全吴胜利出席]," *PLA Daily* [解放军报], September 26, 2012.

Pellerin, Cheryl, "Haney: Strategic Deterrence More Than a Nuclear Triad," Washington, D.C.: U.S. Department of Defense, January 15, 2015. As of October 13, 2015:
http://www.defense.gov/news/newsarticle.aspx?id=123981

Peng Guangqian and Yao Youzhi [彭光谦，姚有志], eds., *The Science of Military Strategy* [战略学], Beijing: Military Science Press [军事科学出版社], 2001.

———, *The Science of Military Strategy,* official English translation of the 2001 Chinese edition, Beijing: Military Science Press, 2005.

People's Liberation Army Military Terms [中国解放军军语], Beijing: Military Science Academy Press [军事科学出版社], December 2011.

Pollpeter, Kevin, "China's Space Robotic Arm Programs," *SITC Bulletin Analysis*, San Diego, Calif.: University of California, San Diego, Institute on Global Conflict and Cooperation, October 2013. As of October 13, 2015:
https://escholarship.org/uc/item/2js0c5r8#page-1

———, "Controlling the Information Domain: Space, Cyber, and Electronic Warfare," in Ashley J. Tellis and Travis Tanner, eds., *Strategic Asia 2012–13: China's Military Challenge*, Seattle, Wa.: National Bureau of Asian Research, October 2012.

Saalman, Lora, "Prompt Global Strike: China and the Spear," Honolulu, Hawaii: Asia-Pacific Center for Security Studies, April 2014. As of October 13, 2015:
http://www.apcss.org/wp-content/uploads/2014/04/APCSS_Saalman_PGS_China_Apr2014.pdf

Schelling, Thomas C., *Arms and Influence*, New Haven, Conn.: Yale University Press, 1966, pp. 69–78.

Shen Di and Hou Guanghua [沈堤, 侯广华], "The Development of Our Nation's Ballistic Missile Defense System Should Insist on the 'Four Establishes' [我国弹道导弹防御系统发展应坚持"四个确立"]," *National Defense Technology* [国防科技], 2012. As of October 13, 2015:
http://lt.cjdby.net/archiver/t-1543664-1-%E6%88%91%E5%9B%BD%E5%BC%B9%E9%81%93%E5%AF%BC%E5%BC%B9%E9%98%B2%E5%BE%A1%E7%B3%BB%E7%BB%9F%E5%8F%91%E5%B1%95%E5%BA%94%E5%9D%9A%E6%8C%81%E2%80%9C%E5%9B%9B%E4%B8%AA%E7%A1%AE%E7%AB%8B%E2%80%9D.html

SMS (2001 and 2005 editions)—*See* Peng Guangqian and Yao Youzhi.

SMS (2013 edition)—*See* Military Strategy Research Department.

SSAC—*See* Li Xianyun et al.

Takahashi, Sugio, "Crafting Deterrence and Defense: The New Defense Policy of Japan," The Tokyo Foundation, October 10, 2012. As of February 15, 2016:
http://www.tokyofoundation.org/en/topics/japan-china-next-generation-dialogue/crafting-deterrence-and-defense

Tellis, Ashley J., "China's Military Space Strategy," *Survival*, Vol. 49, No. 3, September 2007, pp. 41–72. As of February 12, 2016:
http://www.tandfonline.com/doi/full/10.1080/00396330701564752

U.S. Department of Defense, *Annual Report to Congress: Military and Security Developments Involving the People's Republic of China 2015*, Washington, D.C.: Office of the Secretary of Defense, May 2015. As of October 13, 2015:
http://www.defense.gov/pubs/2015_China_Military_Power_Report.pdf

U.S. Navy, *The PLA Navy: New Capabilities and Missions for the 21st Century*, Washington, D.C.: Office of Naval Intelligence (ONI), 2015. As of February 12, 2016:
http://http://www.oni.navy.mil/Portals/12/Intel%20agencies/China_Media/2015_PLA_NAVY_PUB_Interactive.pdf?ver=2015-12-02-081058-483

Weeden, Brian, "Through a Glass, Darkly: Chinese, American, and Russian Anti-Satellite Testing in Space," Broomfield, Colo.: Secure World Foundation, March 17, 2014. As of October 13, 2015:
http://swfound.org/media/167224/Through_a_Glass_Darkly_March2014.pdf

Xu Qi [徐起], *On Military-Civilian Compatible Support System* [军民兼容保障系统论], Beijing: National Defense University Press [国防大学出版社], 2001.

Yang Xuejun, Zhang Wangxin, Shui Jing, Wang Tianzhong, Ren Dexin, Zou Hanbing, Wu Min, and Guo Ping, *Advantage Comes From Space: The Space Battlefield and Space Operations* [优势来自空间—论空间战场与空间作战], Beijing: Guofang gongye chubanshe, 2006.

Ye Zheng [叶征], "On Essential Characteristics, Force Composition and Content Form of Strategic Competition in Cyberspace [论网络空间战略博弈的本质特征，力量构成与内容形式]," People.cn, Theory Channel [人民网－理论频道], August 18, 2014. As of October 13, 2015: http://theory.pcople.com.cn/n/2014/0818/c40531-25487795.html

Yue Guiyun, Chen Xiaoyang, and Li Jingxu, "Considerations on Some Important Issues on New Joint Operations in the Future [未来新型联合作战若干重要问题思考]," *China Military Science* [中国军事科学], 2012.

Zhang Wannian, *Biography of Zhang Wannian* [张万年传], Beijing: PLA Press, 2011.

Zhao Xijun [赵锡君], ed., *Intimidation Warfare: A Comprehensive Discussion of Missile Deterrence* [慑战: 导弹威慑纵横谈], Beijing: National Defense University Press [国防大学出版社], 2005.

Zhu Hui, ed., *Strategic Air Force* [战略空军论], Beijing: Blue Sky Press, 2009.